Mastering
Point of View

SHERRI SZEMAN

STORY PRESS
CINCINNATI, OHIO
www.writersdigest.com

A version of chapter 11, under the title "Urgency: Good Fiction Needs It," © Sherri Szeman, originally appeared in *The Writer* January 1996 and was reprinted in *The 1997 Writer's Handbook*.

A version of chapter 12, under the title "No Demons, No Saints: Creating Realistic Characters," © Sherri Szeman, originally appeared in *The Writer* November 1996.

Visit our Web site at http://www.writersdigest.com for information on more resources for writers.

To receive a free weekly e-mail newsletter delivering tips and updates about writing and about Writer's Digest products, register directly at our Web site at http://www.writersdigest.com.

05 04 03 02 01   5 4 3 2 1

Library of Congress Cataloging-in-Publication Data

Szeman, Sherri
    Mastering point of view / by Sherri Szeman.—1st ed.
        p.   cm.
    Includes bibliographical references and index.
    ISBN 1-884910-52-1
        1. Fiction—Technique. 2. Point of view (Literature). I. Title.

    PN3383.P64 S94   2001
    808.3—dc21   2001035502
                                                              CIP

Edited by Meg Leder and Jack Heffron
Production edited by Donya Dickerson
Designed by Angela Wilcox
Production coordinated by John Peavler

For Tom
and
for Connie

Think where man's glory most begins and ends,
And say my glory was I had such friends.

WILLIAM BUTLER YEATS
"The Municipal Gallery Revisited"

ACKNOWLEDGMENTS

Grateful acknowledgment is made to Tom Gannon and Connie Post, both of whom read the manuscript in draft and provided valuable criticism and feedback. To Sharon Brown and Michael Neeman, who helped me when I researched some of the commercial fiction.

To Becky Keller, Barbara Walker, Mary McGuire, Michelle Burch, Christopher Williams, Terrence Glass, Sharon Brown and Evelyn Schott, whose love, faith and moral support always surround me.

To Judy Pistilli for all her encouragement, faith and love over the years. To Sonja Bond-Clark and Linda Vanarsdall, who straighten out my body after long days of writing and typing.

To my agents, Jennifer Hengen and Neeti Madan, with much gratitude, affection and respect. To my editors, Jack Heffron, for first getting the idea for the book, and to Meg Leder, for her incredible support, insightful suggestions and excellent critical feedback.

To my husband, Tom, who always listens no matter how long I talk about writing. And to Spike, Zoë, Vinnie, Hannah and Zeke, who lie on the computer monitor or the desk and keep me company every day when I write.

ABOUT THE AUTHOR

Sherri Szeman's first novel, *The Kommandant's Mistress*, was awarded the University of Rochester's 1994 Janet Heidinger Kafka Prize for "outstanding work of fiction written by an American woman" and was chosen as one of the *New York Times Book Review's* Best Books of 1993. It is being developed into a film starring Patrick Stewart. She is a professor of English literature and creative writing whose poetry and short fiction appear regularly in literary and university journals across the country.

Books by Sherri Szeman
  Only With the Heart
  The Kommandant's Mistress

CONTENTS

ONE

WHO'S AFRAID OF POINT OF VIEW?

Narrative, like beauty, is in the mind's eye of the beholder.

GARRETT STEWART

Dear Reader: The Conscripted Audience in Nineteenth-Century British Fiction

Wanna see something scary? Take a look at a few of the terms floating around in creative writing handbooks to explain point of view: viewpoint character, focus character, referential and nonreferential narrative, psycho-narration, subjective narration, overt or covert narration, anonymous narration from multiple character point of view, zero focalization, implied or self-effaced author. It's enough to make you shudder. It's no wonder that many creative writers are confused about point of view in fiction.

It doesn't help to turn to literary criticism either. Some critics argue, for example, that every story is told by a narrator, even fairy tales and folktales, which start with "once upon a time." Though it's true that the technical definition of the term *narrator* is "one who tells a story" and the author is, indeed, the one telling the story, popular and traditional usage limits the term *narrator* to an "I" or "we" in the story, whether as an active participant, like Huck in Mark Twain's *The Adventures of Huckleberry Finn*, or as an observer, like Nick in F. Scott Fitzgerald's *The Great Gatsby*.

Literary critics claim that "third-person narrators" stand completely outside the story they're telling, speaking of the participants within the story in the grammatical third person, using he, she, it, they. As if that weren't confusing enough to someone trying to understand literary point of view, some critics complicate the situation even further by presenting terms like *heterodiegetic narrator* and *homodiegetic narrator*, as Gérard Genette did in

Narrative Discourse: An Essay in Method and *Narrative Discourse Revisited*. Knowing that those terms were based on Plato's terms for *authorial discourse* (diegesis), which is differentiated from the *imitated speech of a character* (mimesis), doesn't make the terms any easier to understand or remember. And it certainly doesn't help creative writers learn how to master point of view.

So, despite rhetorician and critic Wayne C. Booth's complaint in *Rhetoric of Fiction* that there are not enough divisions or distinctions to point of view, most writers still understand the more limited terms with which many of us grew up:

- first-person point of view, with an "I" or a "we" telling the story
- third-person unlimited, also known as the omniscient point of view since the author is considered godlike, written in grammatical third person: he, she, it, they
- third-person limited, one version of which is also called the fly-on-the-wall or the camera point of view, also in grammatical third person
- second-person point of view, addressing a "you," which is sometimes the reader

THE ESSENTIAL GUIDE TO POINT OF VIEW

The purpose of this book is not to add any more divisions or complicated terms to the study of point of view. Nor is it to analyze the author's motive behind his choice of point of view or to pass judgment on the quality of any individual point of view. Instead, it is to offer practical advice for creative writers, especially novelists, on mastering point of view.

Exploring the historical development of point of view in literary fiction (appendix A), modern and contemporary novels (appendix B) and commercial fiction (appendix C) can help you learn about point of view. Excerpts from classical works and explorations into the author's choice of point of view as well as how and why it works, all of which can be found in this book, can help you examine your own work and bring you to a fuller understanding of point of view. Most of the chapters in this book end with exercises designed to help you explore point of view on your own, and many of the exercises provide evaluation tools so that you can measure your own progress in mastering point of view.

If you are a beginning writer, you may have many questions about how to conquer this rather intimidating territory, and this book will answer them. If you are an accomplished writer, you can explore the already familiar terrain by learning about writers with whom you may not be familiar. You can also develop your skills in ways you have not previously done by writing in a point of view you have never chosen before and by doing the exercises provided.

TIP Read novels that are considered classics in their point of view (many of these are listed in the appendices). Read with a critical eye, that is, with a conscious awareness of the point-of-view techniques the author is using. Several questions and exercises are provided in the chapters to guide you in your exploration of point of view. Develop your own appreciation and intuitive understanding by reading and writing different points of view.

WHY POINT OF VIEW IS IMPORTANT TO NOVELISTS

Most nonfiction writing does not trouble itself with point of view. Mostly, these works are written in the voices of their authors or in unlimited point of view, where the author provides all the information her readers may need. Poetry concerns itself with point of view (and voice) most often in dramatic monologues, like T.S. Eliot's "The Love Song of J. Alfred Prufrock" and "The Journey of the Magi" or like Robert Browning's "My Last Duchess," in which the voice of the first-person narrator is so distinctive that it develops his character. In fiction, however, point of view is vitally important. It can completely alter the reader's experience of the characters and events that take place. Examine these classic opening lines:

- All happy families resemble one another, but each unhappy family is unhappy in its own way (*Anna Karenina*, by Leo Tolstoy).

- You don't know about me, without you have read a book by the name of "The Adventures of Tom Sawyer," but that ain't no matter (*The Adventures of Huckleberry Finn*, by Mark Twain).
- Dear Father and Mother: I have great trouble, and some comfort, to acquaint you with (*Pamela: Or Virtue Rewarded*, by Samuel Richardson).
- Miss Brooke had that kind of beauty which seems to be thrown into relief by poor dress (*Middlemarch*, by George Eliot).
- Alexey Fyodorovitch Karamazov was the third son of Fyodor Pavlovitch Karamazov, a landowner well known in our district in his own day, and still remembered among us owing to his gloomy and tragic death, which happened thirteen years ago, and which I shall describe in its proper place (*The Brothers Karamazov*, by Fyodor Dostoevsky).
- I had the story, bit by bit, from various people, and, as generally happens in such cases, each time it was a different story (*Ethan Frome*, by Edith Wharton).

Imagine, for a moment, these lines written from a different point of view. Change the opening of Eliot's *Middlemarch* from unlimited to first person: "I have that kind of beauty which seems to be thrown into relief by poor dress." What a different opinion we have of Miss Dorothea Brooke if it is her voice rather than an omniscient author's that describes her beauty. Likewise, changing Twain's *The Adventures of Huckleberry Finn* from first person completely eliminates the distinct and unique voice of his narrator-protagonist. Change the point of view of Dostoevsky's *The Brothers Karamazov* or Wharton's *Ethan Frome*, and we lose the delicious thrill and intimacy of hearing a neighbor, friend or family member relate someone else's secret and tragic history.

It is not an exaggeration to say that a novel *is* its point of view, for point of view determines the readers' responses, controls the readers' sympathies or empathies for the characters, and engages or distances the readers' emotional involvement in the fictional world. Without point of view, we lose the rich texture and sheen of fiction's fabric. Without point of view, we do not have engaging, disturbing or memorable fiction. In novels, point of view is even more important than it is in short stories and novellas, if only because of the more extensive world the author is creating. Point of view can help you create your fictional world more realistically and make your characters more alive for your audience, so it is essential to understand and master point of view.

WHAT POINT OF VIEW IS *NOT*

Point of view is not determined by the main character, whether you call him protagonist, antagonist, viewpoint character, focal character or implied author. Point of view is not determined by any characters, no matter which of them the novel focuses on. Point of view is not determined by setting, time period or atmosphere, nor is it determined by whether or not the author's personal beliefs in any way correspond with those expressed in the novel (by characters in thoughts, monologues or dialogue, or by an omniscient voice in unlimited point of view).

Point of view is not regulated by whether the characters are speaking to themselves, to some specific listener or to a more nebulous and distant audience. It is not based on a narrator's reliability or unreliability, participation in or observation of the events related. Point of view is not themes, symbolism or political agendas disguised as fiction. Point of view is not determined by whether the author shows or tells, by whether the characters are round, flat, evolving or static. Point of view is not determined by the novel's genre, be it fantasy, science fiction, mystery, suspense, romance, Western or literary fiction. All genres have examples of novels written in each of the various points of view.

WHAT IS POINT OF VIEW?

So what is point of view? Most simply stated, it's how the novel is written.

That's all there is to it. How the book is written.

HOW MANY POINTS OF VIEW ARE THERE?

So just how many points of view are there? For simplicity's sake, we are going to concentrate on the traditional divisions with a few distinctions for clarification: first, second, unlimited, outer limited, inner limited and combo.

- **First person:** If there's an "I" or a "we" telling the story, then a narrator is present, and the book is written in first-person point of view. The narrator may be reliable or unreliable, but in either case, the events in the novel are limited to what the narrator can observe and to the narrator's psychological and emotional life (more on that in chapter 3).
- **Second person:** If someone is directly addressed as "you" (and not in dialogue), then second-person point of view is being used. This directly addressed "you" may be the readers themselves; humanity in general; other actual or implied characters in the novel; or specific historical, political or otherwise famous people outside the novel who are not the readers (see chapter 5).
- **Unlimited:** If the author uses he, she, it or they and tells the reader everything in every character's head and heart, then the novel is written in unlimited point of view, which has also been called third-person point of view or the omniscient point of view, since the author has been likened to an all-knowing creator God in the Judeo-Christian tradition. The author reveals every character's thoughts, feelings, motivations and actions. This is the only point of view not limited in some fashion, hence its name (see chapter 2).
- **Outer limited:** The point of view is outer limited if the author uses the grammatical third person but does not present an unlimited view of the characters, choosing instead to show only the external, observable behaviors and dialogue of all of his characters, for example, as Ernest Hemingway and Alain Robbe-Grillet do. This is also known as the fly-on-the-wall or the camera point of view since it never presents characters' interior, psychological or emotional lives (see chapter 6).
- **Inner limited:** If the author shows the thoughts and feelings of one character as if she were in that character's head, though still writing in the grammatical third person, using he, she or it to refer to the character whose thoughts and feelings she's revealing, and presents only the external observations of the other characters, as James Joyce and Henry

James often do, then the point of view is inner limited. This point of view is exactly like first person but is written in the grammatical third person (see chapter 4).

- **Combo:** If the author is writing commercial fiction, especially suspense or crime mysteries, and uses unlimited point of view when focusing on the crime-fighting protagonists but uses inner limited point of view when focusing on the victims or criminals, then the author is using combo point of view, which has been recognized as its own category (sometimes called limited omniscience) by the critics (see chapter 7).

Variations on Point of View

How many combinations of these basic points of view are there? Millions. How many subtle shadings exist within these points of view? Maybe billions. But you don't have to count them all to use them. You don't even have to be aware of all the variations and combinations to master point of view.

WHY ALL THE CONFUSION ABOUT POINT OF VIEW?

In everyday conversation, we use the term *point of view* to refer to different sides of a situation. For example, if there's an accident and a police officer questions three people and gets three different versions of what happened, we say that he gets three different points of view. If we're having a heated discussion with someone who disagrees with us, we say, "That's your point of view." Each time we hear someone else's version of events, we say we have a different point of view.

In literature and creative writing, however, point of view is limited to how the fiction is written. So if the police officer in the previous example hears three first-person narratives about the accident, then—in literary and creative writing terms—he's heard three stories from the same point of view: first person. Each of these first-person narratives, though, is from a different perspective. So, in literary terms, the police officer has heard three perspectives from the same point of view. That distinction is critical for creative writers if they wish to master point of view.

Different Perspective, Same Point of View

An author can change perspective without changing point of view. Here are two scenes from my novel, *Only With the Heart*, that illustrate a change in perspective while maintaining the same point of view. Each is told in first person, so there is no change in point of view from a literary standpoint. Since each narrator is giving a different version of what happened, however, there are two different perspectives. In this first scene, from the third chapter of part 3, Sam, one of the novel's three narrators, is putting away a baby cradle and an unfinished rocking horse after his wife, Claudia, has had yet another miscarriage.

> Our dream of having kids was dead. After the last miscarriage, the doctor told Claudia to give up trying. He told her she was risking her own life with every pregnancy. That's why I put all the baby furniture up in the attic. . . . I went out to the hall with the baby furniture and carried it up to the attic. I set the cradle and rocking horse down under the eaves, next to the bassinet, the changing table, and the dresser. When I stepped back, dust swirled around in the sunlight and made me cough. I picked up some of the old blankets, shook them out, and tucked them around the baby's furniture. Those blankets were so big, and that cradle was so small. And it would never hold a baby. It was small and dead and empty. Like my life.

Sam was not aware that his mother, Eleanor, was watching him while he moved the baby furniture into the attic. In the corresponding scene in Eleanor's section of the novel (part 2, chapter 4), Eleanor, who is terminally ill with Alzheimer's, also describes Sam's putting the rocking horse and cradle into the attic. Since Eleanor has Alzheimer's, she doesn't remember the words for the items of furniture that her son is moving. She describes his emotional reaction to the event—something Sam neglects to do in his version of the story—and she, too, is upset, but she is unable to comfort him as he weeps over the loss of his unborn child.

> He doesn't see me. He goes past my room with it. I go after him. He goes up the stairs. To the top of the house. No one

else is with him. He takes it to the corner. The sun shines on it. He makes his fingers go along the wood. When he touches it, it rocks. He wipes his face with his hand. He makes the blanket go all around it. But he doesn't get up. He stays next to it. On the floor. He puts his hands over his face. His shoulders shake. He makes a funny noise. . . . He makes that noise over and over. No one hears him. No one but me.

Since these two sections are both told from first-person point of view, there is no change in the point of view. We do, however, have a change in perspective since we have two different narrators telling the event as they remember it.

Different Focus, Same Point of View

Beginning writers also often think that describing different characters is changing point of view; so if one paragraph is about Charles, the next about Emma and the third about Rodolphe, they believe that the author has changed point of view. If the author has written about Charles, Emma and Rodolphe in unlimited point of view, however, and not varied from that, then the author has not changed point of view. He has changed his focus from one character to another but not how he has written about them.

The following excerpt, from the first chapter of Alexandre Dumas's *The Three Musketeers*, is a description of the protagonist, D'Artagnan, written in unlimited point of view, which is always in the grammatical third person.

A young man . . . a Don Quixote of eighteen . . . clothed in a woolen doublet, the blue color of which had faded into a nameless shade between lees of wine and a heavenly azure; face long and brown, high cheek-bones; . . . the eye open and intelligent; the nose hooked, but finely chiseled. Too big for a youth, too small for a grown man, an experienced eye might have taken him for a farmer's son upon a journey, had it not been for the long sword. . . .

Later in that chapter, when D'Artagnan meets a stranger who insults him, Dumas—still using unlimited point of view—changes focus but maintains the same point of view.

> Nevertheless, D'Artagnan was desirous of examining the appearance of this impertinent personage who was laughing at him. He fixed his haughty eye upon the stranger, and perceived a man of from forty to forty-five years of age, with black and piercing eyes, a pale complexion, a strongly-marked nose, and a black and well-shaped mustache. He was dressed in a doublet and hose of a violet color. . . .

Though the author has shifted his focus in order to describe different characters, he has not shifted how he has written about them, so he has not changed point of view.

Different Points of View

An author can change her focus, describing different characters, without changing her point of view. She can change perspective, giving different versions of the same story, without changing point of view. It is only when an author changes from first (I, we) to second (you), first to unlimited (he, she, it, they), etc., that she is changing point of view.

Henry Fielding does this in his masterpiece, *Tom Jones*, moving frequently from unlimited, in which the bulk of the novel is written; to first, in which he calls attention to himself as the author; to second, in which he directly addresses his audience. Here is an excerpt from the opening paragraph from book 1, chapter 2, written in unlimited point of view:

> In that part of the western division of this kingdom which is commonly called Somersetshire, there lately lived and perhaps lives still, a gentleman whose name was Allworthy. . . . From [Nature] he derived an agreeable person, a sound constitution, a sane understanding, and a benevolent heart; by [Fortune], he was decreed to the inheritance of one of the largest estates in the county.

At the end of that chapter, Fielding switches from unlimited to first and second, as he will continue to do throughout the novel.

> Reader, I think proper, before we proceed any farther together, to acquaint thee that I intend to digress, through

this whole history, as often as I see occasion, of which I am myself a better judge than any pitiful critic whatever; and here I must desire all those critics to mind their own business, and not to intermeddle with affairs or works which no ways concern them. . . .

William Faulkner's masterpiece of different perspectives as well as multiple points of view, *The Sound and the Fury*, is divided into four sections, the first three of which are all in first-person point of view and the last of which is in unlimited. So his novel has two different points of view: first and unlimited. The first three sections, all first-person narratives, provide three different perspectives, but the author does not change point of view.

My novel, *The Kommandant's Mistress*, is divided into three sections; but the first two, though giving different perspectives on the story, are both written in first-person point of view. Here is a scene (from part 1, chapter 6) in which the Kommandant is at his desk writing something late at night, from his perspective:

> When the words wouldn't come, I pulled off my ring, the silver band with the death's head and the *heil* rune, and turned it over and over in my left hand while I worked. . . . The words came. I slipped the ring back on. I saw the girl, watching me.

Since Rachel, the Jewish inmate he forces to be his mistress, is kept prisoner in his office, she is often able to tell the reader things that happen there. Here again (in part 2, chapter 5) is the scene with the Kommandant writing, this time from the girl's perspective. Note that since it is also in first person, there is no change in point of view.

> Often, he worked all night. The light kept me awake. I lay on the cot he had brought down and watched him. When his pen stopped, he pulled off his ring. Not his wedding ring. He never took that off. The silver band with the death's head. . . . When he saw me watching, he stopped writing.

The Kommandant does not tell us what he's writing, and the girl doesn't know, so she cannot tell us.

In the third section of the novel, written in a different point of view—unlimited, which is in the grammatical third person—we learn at last what the Kommandant has been writing in his office in the middle of the night.

> By the time the Allies liberated the camp, [Kommandant] von Walther had already fled. His home and office, however, located on the camp's grounds, were virtually intact, and a great many incriminating documents were recovered. Among these were two complete manuscripts of verse, discovered under the floorboards of his office. Though the poems in these manuscripts are filled with intimate details of von Walther's personal and professional life, the handwriting of these manuscripts does not exactly match that on the other documents alleged to have been written by von Walther, so it is highly unlikely that the poems were written by him.

Notice that I am not analyzing the reliability of this passage in terms of what it reveals about the Kommandant (for example, when it says "the handwriting of these manuscripts does not exactly match that on the other documents alleged to have been written by von Walther, so it is highly unlikely that the poems were written by him"). It does not affect point of view if the fictional writer of this biographical entry on the Kommandant is inaccurate in his interpretation of the facts.

What is important for our purposes here is the change in point of view. The point of view in the first two sections of the novel, since they are both written in first person, does not change. Since this final section of the novel switches from first person to unlimited, however, it *is* a change in point of view.

POINT OF VIEW, FOCUS AND PERSPECTIVE

Point of view, then, is how the book is written, not who or what it is about. When the author describes different characters or settings but does not change how he is writing about them, then he is changing focus but maintaining the same point of view. You can change the direction the camera is pointing—focus—or you can switch from black-and-white to color film—perspective—but to change point of view, you would have to change the camera from a video camera to an 8mm camera. Changing point of view changes the author's experience of the novel as well as the readers'.

When the author gives us different versions of the same events, perhaps all written in first-person point of view, for example, then he is giving us different perspectives, but he is not changing point of view. Only if the author writes one section of the novel in first person, with a narrator using "I" or "we" to tell the story, and another in unlimited, using "he," "she," "it" or "they" to tell the story and moving freely both inside and outside all the characters' heads (or writing any sections of the novel in any combination of multiple points of view), is the author actually changing literary point of view. Clarity about the difference between literary point of view, common usage of the term point of view, focus and perspective will make your task easier when you write your novel.

MYTHS ABOUT POINT OF VIEW

Critics (and some writers) love to make up rules about writing in general and about point of view in particular, perhaps because it is a challenging area to master and even the best authors sometimes make mistakes in point of view. But many of these "rules" have attained an almost mythic status; they are passed out at writers' conferences as if the rules were carved in stone and handed down at Mt. Sinai.

Inexperienced writers are often told that if they don't follow the mythical rules about point of view, they'll never get published, the equivalent of telling an aspiring author that he will be spending the rest of his life in hell. But I've learned that most of these rules are just myths and that you can always find reputable, well-written books that successfully break the traditional conventions concerning point of view.

Let's examine some of these myths:

Myth #1: Commercial fiction (also called formula or genre fiction, such as mysteries, romances, science fiction, etc.) is always written in unlimited point of view.

This is simply not true. An exploration of the classic books of commercial fiction reveals as many books written in first person as in unlimited point of view.

Myth #2: Literary fiction is always written in first-person point of view.

I'm not sure how this myth got started, unless the person who said it meant to say that contemporary literary fiction is always written in first-person point of view, but even that's not true. Although there is a great deal of contemporary literary fiction written in first person, there is also a great deal written in unlimited, inner limited and outer limited points of view.

Myth #3: You can't write from a man's perspective if you're a woman (or vice versa), even if you're using first-person point of view.

There is a long history of male authors who are unable to create realistic female characters, Shakespeare and Hemingway among them, as well as an equally long list of female authors whose male characters are not considered realistic, no matter what point of view their books are written in. Nevertheless, there are many fine examples of male authors writing in first person as a female character, such as Arthur Golden's *Memoirs of a Geisha*, and of female authors writing in first person as a male character, as I did in both of my novels, *The Kommandant's Mistress* and *Only With the Heart*, and as Joyce Carol Oates does in *Zombie*.

The author's gender does not matter as much as the author's willingness to enter into the thoughts, feelings, desires and motivations of his character, and the author's ability to separate himself from the character he is creating (more on that in chapter 10).

Myth #4: You can't switch point of view in a novel. You must pick one point of view and stay with it throughout the book.

There is a difference between switching point of view and lapsing from your chosen point of view. Lapsing means you've erroneously slipped out of the point of view you've chosen, and that's simply a writing mistake.

But not switching point of view? Of course you can. How often? That depends on the work itself and on your skill as a writer. (There's more on switching points of view in chapter 9.)

Myth #5: Each time you describe a different character, you are changing point of view.

This is not true unless you also go from first person to unlimited (or vice versa) or from any point of view to another. Simply changing the focus of your writing does not change your point of view.

Myth #6: First-person point of view is easier to write than the others.

At first glance, this might seem to be true. But if you're really faithful to the character's perspective, as opposed to your own, writing in first person, because it is always a limited point of view, can be extremely difficult and demanding. The challenges of first person increase exponentially if you're using unreliable narrators (see chapters 3 and 8). In fact, I would venture to say that first person is one of the more challenging points of view.

Myth #7: It's easy to write in outer limited point of view because you're pretending you're a camera, so you just write down everything you see.

Outer limited is, without a doubt, the most difficult point of view in which to write. Even if you pretend you're a camera or a fly on the wall, as Ernest Hemingway described this point of view, it's much more demanding than it seems. As a camera or a fly on the wall, you must remain absolutely objective, nonjudgmental and nonhuman. Your emotions as the author must not be revealed in this point of view. Whether or not you like or approve of your characters and their actions must not be revealed. After all, you are a camera or a fly.

As a human writer, however, every single word you choose is subjective and can reveal your emotions and judgment on the scenes you are writing. That's what causes the problems and the difficulties in this point of view. Outer limited is the most difficult point of view to use successfully, and it's the one authors most often lapse in (see more in chapters 6 and 10).

Myth #8: Even if you're writing fiction, you can only write about aspects of your own life from your own perspective. Otherwise, you're "trespassing" into other people's lives and experiences.

If this were true, then most of the world's fiction—literary and commercial—would be eliminated. How many bald, midget, alternate-world doctors (*Insomnia*) do you think Stephen King has met? How many serial killers has Patricia Cornwell (*Postmortem*) encountered in her bedroom? And if you only write your own life, then you're writing memoir or autobiography, not fiction.

Fiction writers have a moral obligation to tell good stories and to write from perspectives other than their own. How would fiction writers ever master first-person point of view if they only wrote about themselves? If they only wrote about their own lives from their own perspective, wouldn't they be writing the same book over and over? And if they were only writing from their own personal and limited perspective, then they'd certainly have a difficult time mastering any of the other points of view.

Myth #9: There are really no limitations to first-person point of view; you can shift to something called "objective narration" and then into unlimited point of view as long as you do it in stages.

Of course, there are no limitations to any point of view if you don't care if you're doing it authentically. The limitations to first-person point of view are the same limitations any human being has: Each of us only knows what's in her own head and heart; everything else is viewed externally. If you're authentically writing in first-person point of view, then you cannot shift to unlimited—no matter how subtly or in how many stages you do it. If you want to tell everything about every character, you should use unlimited point of view. If you want to write in first person, then you need to accept the fact that there are real limitations.

Myth #10: Famous writers like James Joyce (in _Ulysses_) often change point of view, sometimes in the middle of a sentence. If they can do it, so can other writers.

It's true that James Joyce shifts point of view in _Ulysses_ often and in the middle of sentences. It's also true that it's confusing and that not many people besides Joyce scholars read _Ulysses_. So if you want to take a chance on having an extremely limited (and possibly confused) audience, then shift point of view as often as you want with no purpose whatsoever. However, if there's a logical and artistic reason for shifting point of view, and you don't want to lose your readers, you can read about successfully using multiple points of view in the same novel (chapter 9).

HOW TO USE THIS BOOK

Chapters 2 through 10 deal with point of view, its definitions and its challenges, including how to choose which point of view is best for your novel. These chapters contain many examples from both literary and commercial fiction, along with advice on how you, too, can master certain aspects of that point of view. Chapters 11 through 14 deal with the other elements of creative writing, such as urgency, dialogue and character development, and their relationship to point of view. Chapter 15 explores how point of view can help you with revision and aid you in eliminating writer's block.

All the chapters provide examples from both literary and commercial fiction, writing tips or exercises designed to help you become a better novelist and to master point of view. The chapters do not have to be read in any particular order, although they do progress from the easier concepts to the more challenging ones—from unlimited point of view to challenging perspectives and multiple points of view, from urgency to symbolism. A glossary has been provided for your convenience in understanding terms.

THE IMPORTANCE OF READERS

Throughout this book, the exercises direct you to show what you've written to readers and get their feedback. This step is vitally important to your success as a writer. Your readers—whether friends, family members, instructors or professional writers—

must be people who can give you informed, literate feedback about your writing. After all, if your readers never say anything except "That's nice," you will not improve as a writer.

I'm not saying that you should instruct your readers to find negative things to say about your work, but you should direct their attention to the specific areas you're working on and ask their assistance in analyzing your skill level in that area. For example, if you are working on creating realistic characters, you might ask your readers how they feel about a particular character, do they understand her behavior, would they want to have her over for Thanksgiving dinner, would they want to be in a relationship with her, would they want to be related to her, etc. If you're working on first-person point of view, you might ask them if they believe that the narrator would really think/say the things you have her thinking/saying.

If your relatives or friends are unable or unwilling to critique your writing, then you can hire professional readers. College or university English department faculty and graduate students will often critique manuscripts for reasonable rates, as will professional evaluators. You can enroll in creative writing classes at colleges or attend some of the numerous creative writing workshops and conferences across the country.

You must find reliable readers to give you critical feedback on your work even if you have to pay for their services. If you're writing in areas in which you're not an expert, such as police or medical procedures, you should contact professionals in the field and engage them as readers. Though they will charge you for this service, you will find it tremendously helpful in writing quality fiction and mastering point of view.

READING LIST

To master point of view, and to write good novels generally, you must also read. Many aspiring writers are familiar with the names of the famous authors but haven't read their works. Few aspiring writers have read outside their own genre, despite the fact that this is one of the surest ways to increase your novel-writing skills in general and to improve your mastery of point of view in particular. For that reason, instead of a reading list indicating only the titles, I have provided a historical overview of the development of point of view in literary and in commercial fiction in the appendices. While it's not essential that you read the appendices, I encourage you to familiarize yourself with the history of point of view in literary and commercial fiction because the historical perspective can show you how a particular point of view has changed or been handled over the years. Also, the appendices can introduce you to many new and exciting authors who can teach you more about point of view by example.

Of course, it was not possible to list every book that has been important in point of view, and I apologize if any of your favorite authors or novels have been excluded. Space prohibited me from mentioning every good novel and quoting from more authors.

YOUR POINT-OF-VIEW JOURNEY

This book can improve your skill as a novelist and help you master point of view. Read both literary and commercial fiction. Read novels that are considered classics in point of view. For your convenience, many of them are discussed in this book. After you've read, you must write. And write. And write some more. It will be an exciting, demanding and thrilling journey. This book will be your companion on that journey.

POINTS OF VIEW

- **First person,** with an "I" or a "we"—a narrator—telling the story; narrators may be reliable or unreliable.
- **Second person,** addressing a "you," which may be the readers themselves; humanity in general; other actual or implied characters in the novel; or specific historical, political or otherwise famous people outside the novel who are not the readers.
- **Unlimited,** also known as the omniscient or "author as God" point of view, written in grammatical third person: he, she, it, they; where every character's thoughts, feelings, motivations and actions are presented; there are no limits to the information an author can reveal. Sometimes presented ambiguously, where multiple possibilities of interpretation for a character's behavior are presented without the author's guidance in selection, as in the work of the postmodernists.

- **Inner limited,** exactly like first person but written in grammatical third person: he, she, it, they; limited to the inner life of one character, with that character's thoughts and feelings revealed and only the external aspects of other characters presented.
- **Outer limited,** also known as the fly-on-the-wall or camera point of view, written in grammatical third person: he, she, it, they; limited to presenting only the observable externals, such as behavior and dialogue, of all characters.

Variations on Point of View

- **Combo,** sometimes called limited omniscient or flexible/revolving third person, written in grammatical third person: he, she, it, they; in which the author moves back and forth among unlimited and inner limited points of view; now sometimes recognized as a distinct category by literary critics and considered conventional in some types of commercial fiction, with unlimited point of view used for the crime-fighting protagonists and inner limited for the victims or the criminals.
- **Multiple,** any combination of different points of view, with sections of the novel (or story) written in completely different points of view, such as a novel that combines first-person sections with unlimited sections, or first and second with unlimited or unlimited with outer limited. Because the combination of unlimited point of view for the crime-fighting protagonists of a novel and inner limited for the victims or the criminals has been recognized as a separate category by critics and become conventional in some crime novels, it is listed above as "Combo" point of view.

TWO

UNLIMITED POINT OF VIEW

It is not surprising to hear practicing novelists report that they have never had any help from critics about point of view.

WAYNE C. BOOTH

The Rhetoric of Fiction

Unlimited point of view, also called omniscient point of view since the author has been likened to the Judeo-Christian God, is the easiest point of view for novelists because, quite literally, there are no restrictions or limitations to the kind of information the author can present. She is not limited to viewing the world from one character's perspective, nor is she prevented from showing the thoughts, feelings and motivations of any of the characters she wishes. In unlimited point of view, the author writes in grammatical third person—using he, she, it, they—and the author can show the inner psychological life of every character in the novel. The author can also openly present her judgments on the characters and their behavior in unlimited point of view.

KNOWING EVERYTHING VS. REVEALING EVERYTHING

There is a difference between the author's *knowing* everything about his characters and *revealing* everything. Mystery writers, for example, probably know who committed the murder or other crime from the time they sit down to write the novel, but they do not reveal it to their readers or to the other characters in the book until the appropriate moment. Unlimited point of view has nothing to do with what the author knows or reveals about his characters. Rather, it is how the author writes about his characters that determines point of view. If the author shows everything about all the characters' interior private lives to his readers, he is writing in unlimited point of view.

UNLIMITED POINT OF VIEW VS. PERSONA

Unlimited point of view also serves the same purpose as the eighteenth century's so-called "intrusive" personae, who interrupted the story to make commentary (see chapter 3 for the distinction between author, persona and narrator). In a subtle way, unlimited point of view reassures the reader that everything in the novel is under the author's control and will turn out reasonably well (and, at least in commercial fiction, according to the conventional formula). By revealing the thoughts, emotions and motivations of every single character in the novel, the author allows the readers to see the author's control over the fictional world. The author, like the Judeo-Christian God, knows everything about the fictional world he has created. Some readers find it more comfortable if an author tells them everything about the characters since the readers may feel reassured that the novel will unfold according to the readers' expectations.

MORAL JUDGMENT IN COMMERCIAL FICTION

In addition to providing reassurance and guidance, unlimited point of view allows the author to make all the moral decisions for the readers in advance but to present these moral decisions in a more sophisticated way than doing so with a persona. For example, in part 2 chapter 11 of *Anna Karenina*, when author Leo Tolstoy compares Anna's adulterous lovemaking with Vronsky to a murder, Tolstoy's moral condemnation of their affair is clear.

In commercial fiction, villains and criminals are rarely presented sympathetically. Using unlimited point of view, the author chooses words with negative connotations when writing about unsavory characters. For example, a character described as "pathetic, isolated, flighty and strident" is not being presented in a kind manner. All of those words have negative connotations, so the readers, whether or not they are consciously aware of the author's moral judgment, are aware on an emotional level. The readers also interpret the character in a less than favorable light. Similarly, heroes or other characters of whom the author approves are described with words having positive connotations. For example, "stalwart, loyal and diligent" might be used to present the protagonist. By using unlimited point of view and choosing words according to their positive or negative connotations, the author is guiding the readers' moral judgments about the novel's characters.

AUTHOR AS GOD

Many critics liken the author who writes in unlimited point of view to God, but what concerns us here is the implication of God as creator—the omnipotent, omniscient, judgmental, moral, Judeo-Christian God, who gives the Ten Commandments and many chapters of rules to govern human behaviors and guide our decisions about such behavior. Unlimited point of view allows the author to give such moral guidance to her readers.

WHY IS UNLIMITED POINT OF VIEW SO PREVALENT?

Novels written in unlimited point of view are extremely easy to read. This may be due to the fact that the author guides the reader in any moral decisions about the characters or to the fact that the author presents all characters' inner and outer lives. Whatever the reason, novels written in unlimited point of view are very popular.

ADVANTAGES OF UNLIMITED POINT OF VIEW

For an author, the advantage of writing in unlimited point of view is that there are literally no restrictions to the information she can present about her characters to her readers. The author can range freely from character to character, giving information both inside and outside all the characters' heads, without any limits whatsoever. That makes this point of view extremely attractive for a writer.

Thematically, this point of view allows the author to make her points most obvious to the readers. No matter which of the countless themes the author wishes to explore in the novel—man's cruelty to man, oppression of women, the power of language, etc.—unlimited point of view allows the author to do so directly.

Many genres of commercial fiction, such as romance, science

fiction and fantasy, depend on the unlimited point of view to present historical, scientific or imaginary details that could not be effectively presented in other points of view. For instance, if an author of a Regency romance used first person with a female narrator, it might seem unusual and might reflect poorly on the narrator's character to have the narrator discuss her gowns in sufficient detail for the readers to picture it. In unlimited point of view, however, the author can describe the gowns as much as she likes. Since this point of view is not limited in any way, this is the only one that allows the author complete freedom in expressing herself.

The advantages of unlimited point of view for the readers is that they do not have to work to figure out the novel or its characters. The author tells the readers everything necessary for them to understand the novel.

DISADVANTAGES OF UNLIMITED POINT OF VIEW

The major disadvantage of writing in unlimited point of view is that the readers may be less emotionally attached to the characters than they would be in other points of view. This may be due to the fact that the author covers all his characters' thoughts and emotions, preventing a deeper emotional attachment to any one of them. Or it may be due to the fact that, at least in commercial fiction, the readers do not have to interpret characters' moral qualities; the readers simply accept the author's judgment, which may prevent a more intense connection to the characters. Novels written in unlimited point of view may be less challenging to read; whether this is an advantage or a disadvantage will depend on the readers' preference.

UNLIMITED POINT OF VIEW IN LITERARY FICTION

Although the trend in twentieth-century literary fiction has tended more toward narratives written in first-person point of view, many novels in the eighteenth and nineteenth centuries were written in unlimited point of view. Here is a passage from chapter 2 of Miguel de Cervantes's *Don Quixote*, "which deals with our imaginative hero's first sally from his home." I have italicized the words or passages that reveal Quixote's inner life or the author's judgment since these things indicate that section is written in unlimited point of view.

> Once these preparations were made he was *anxious* to put his designs into operation without delay, *for he was spurred on by the conviction* that the world needed his immediate presence; so many were the grievances he *intended* to rectify, the wrongs he *resolved* to set right, the harms he *meant* to redress, the abuses he would reform, and the debts he would discharge. And so, *without appointing a living soul with his intentions, and wholly unobserved*, one morning before daybreak (it was one of the hottest in the month of July), he armed himself cap-a-pie, mounted Rozinante, placed his *ill-constructed* helmet on his head, braced on his buckler, grasped his lance, and through the door of his backyard sallied forth into the open country, *mightily pleased to note* the ease with which he had begun his worthy enterprise.

Cervantes also gives us the thoughts of the other characters, as he does later in chapter 2 when Quixote encounters an innkeeper and tells the innkeeper to stable and to

> . . . take great care of his horse, saying he was one of the finest pieces of horseflesh that ever ate bread. The innkeeper looked [the horse] over and *thought* him not so good by half as his master had said.

Since Cervantes gives us the innkeeper's thoughts, as well as Quixote's in the earlier passage, he is writing in unlimited point of view. Whenever the author writes in the grammatical third person and provides the thoughts, feelings, motivations or interior lives of all the characters, the author is writing in unlimited point of view.

UNLIMITED POINT OF VIEW
IN COMMERCIAL FICTION

Unlimited point of view is extremely popular in commercial fiction. It is so popular, in fact, that there's a myth that commercial fiction can only be written in this point of view (see myth #1 in chapter 1). When an author of commercial fiction uses unlimited point of view, he writes in the grammatical third person and presents the inner lives of all of the characters, just as is done in literary fiction. Here's an example from chapter 1 of *Original Sin* by P.D. James. Again, I have italicized the words or passages that reveal the character's inner life or the author's judgment because these things indicate it is written in unlimited point of view.

> For a temporary shorthand-typist to be present at the discovery of a corpse on the first day of a new assignment, *if not unique, is sufficiently rare to prevent its being regarded as an occupational hazard.* Certainly Mandy Price, aged nineteen years two months, and the acknowledged star of Mrs. Crealey's Nonesuch Secretarial Agency, set out on the morning of Tuesday 14 September for her interview at the Peverell Press *with no more apprehension than she usually felt* at the start of a new job, *an apprehension which was never acute and was rooted less in any anxiety whether she would satisfy the expectations of the prospective employer than in whether the employer would satisfy hers.*

Unlimited point of view is also popular in the Western genre, as this excerpt from the opening of Louis L'Amour's *The Shadow Riders* indicates, when L'Amour gives us the thoughts of the protagonist and his men. Italics indicate the characters' inner lives or the author's presentation of information from the character's past.

> Hunching his shoulders against the cold, pelting rain, Major Mac Traven slipped a hand under his caped coat *to assure himself* his spare pistol remained in position. A sudden gust of wind rattled rain upon his campaign hat and spattered his face and hands. *Desperately tired and carrying the gnawing hunger from three missed meals*, he glanced back along the road at the scattered travelers.

Many other commercial novels are written in unlimited point of view, including Ian Fleming's *Casino Royale*, in the spy-espionage genre, in which the author uses unlimited point of view to reveal inner thoughts and also to guide the readers in their view of his protagonist, James Bond. Other examples of unlimited point of view in commercial fiction include Tom Clancy's *The Hunt for Red October*, Kathleen E. Woodiwiss's *The Wolf and the Dove*, Tony Hillerman's *Listening Woman*, Jude Deveraux's *A Knight in Shining Armor*, Ken Follett's *The Key to Rebecca*, Julie Garwood's *The Bride* and Dean Koontz's *Intensity*.

Whether you're writing Westerns, espionage, romances or literary fiction, if you write in the grammatical third person and provide your readers access to the thoughts, feelings and unspoken motivations of all of the characters, then you are using unlimited point of view.

LIMITED OMNISCIENCE

In the last several years, there has been a growing trend in commercial fiction crime novels to present the criminal or victim in inner limited point of view, that is, limited to the inner life of one character, and to present the protagonist crime-fighters in unlimited point of view. This combo point of view has been called "limited omniscience" by the critics; this combination of points of view has become accepted and conventional in some types of commercial fiction, so it has sometimes been categorized as a distinct type of point of view (see chapter 7 for more information on combo point of view).

EPIGRAPHS AND TITLES

Epigraphs and titles guide the reader in an interpretation of the work. Therefore, epigraphs and titles are considered to be in unlimited point of view no matter what point of view the novel is written in. Authors control the epigraphs they choose, but they do not always make the final decisions regarding the novels' titles. Sometimes titles are chosen by editors or agents for marketing purposes. Still, whether chosen by the author, agent or editor, the title is meant to guide the reader in an interpretation of the novel.

ANIMAL AND NONHUMAN NARRATIVES

Animal and nonhuman narratives can be written in any point of view. These narratives can focus on the animals or they can be told from the animals' own perspective. Here is the opening

---

TIP Some published authors have told tales of how they never quite got used to the title of their novel, which was chosen by an editor, because the author always called it something else previous to its being sold. So don't worry about your novel's title too much. You can always depend on your agent or your editor to help find a more marketable title.

---

paragraph of Jack London's *The Call of the Wild*, written in unlimited point of view. Italicized words or passages indicate unlimited point of view.

> Buck did not read the newspapers, *or he would have known that trouble was brewing, not alone for himself, but for every Tidewater dog*, strong of muscle and with warm, long hair, from Puget Sound to San Diego.

London also uses unlimited point of view for his animal narrative *White Fang*, where he reveals the emotions of a wolf, the sled dogs being observed and the human characters in the novel.

Animal narratives can also present the animals with human characteristics, as a kind of fable or parable for human behavior. George Orwell did this in *Animal Farm*. All the animals take over the farm and try to establish a socialist society. The pigs, however, begin to rule the farm. As this excerpt from chapter 10 shows, the pigs even go so far as to change the seven commandments to a single commandment: "All animals are equal but some animals are more equal than others." Once again, the italics indicate unlimited point of view.

> After that *it did not seem strange* when next day the pigs who were supervising the work of the farm all carried whips in their trotters. *It did not seem strange to learn that the pigs had bought themselves a wireless set, were arranging to install a telephone, and had taken out subscriptions [to newspapers]*. . . .

Animal narratives could also be written in other points of view. For example, you could write the narrative in first-person point of view from the animal's perspective, in first person from a human's perspective, etc. If you choose to write an animal narrative, you should familiarize yourself with the animal so that the details will be realistic.

Nonhuman objects can also be characters in novels, as are Dirty Sock, Can o' Beans and Spoon in Tom Robbins's *Skinny Legs and All*. If using a nonhuman object as your protagonist, you should also be extremely familiar with that object.

STREAM OF CONSCIOUSNESS IN UNLIMITED POINT OF VIEW

In stream-of-consciousness narration, you are attempting to render the thought processes of your characters, including memories and sense perceptions as well as thoughts, in a continuous "stream." Contrary to what you might believe, stream-of-consciousness passages do not have to be written in first-person point of view. In fact, some of the classic examples of stream-of-consciousness have been written in unlimited point of view. Virginia Woolf, in her novel *Mrs. Dalloway*, provides several stream-of-consciousness passages for her characters.

> Indeed, his own life was a miracle; let him make no mistake about it; here he was, in the prime of life, walking to his house in Westminster to tell Clarissa that he loved her. Happiness is this, he thought. It is this, he said, as he entered the dean's yard. . . . Lunch parties wasted the entire afternoon, he thought, approaching his door.

Later on that page, we are presented with Clarissa's stream of consciousness as she ponders all the dull women in London. If Woolf had presented only one character's inner life and feelings in this novel and shown us only the external lives of all the remaining characters, the point of view in this novel would have been inner limited. Since Woolf shows us the inner lives of all her characters, its point of view is unlimited. She uses the stream-of-consciousness technique to give us their inner lives.

As long as you present your character's thoughts, memories, sense perceptions, etc. in a "stream" format, then you can use unlimited point of view to write stream-of-consciousness passages.

Many writers have done just that, including Virginia Woolf in *Mrs. Dalloway* (as noted on the previous page) and *To the Lighthouse* and Henry James in *The Ambassadors* and *The Portrait of a Lady*. (See chapter 3 for stream-of-consciousness passages in first-person point of view.)

TIP Use stream-of-consciousness technique in unlimited point of view if you want to reveal the inner psychological lives of all of your characters, including their unconscious motivations and desires.

AMBIGUOUS UNLIMITED POINT OF VIEW

To learn about ambiguities within points of view, which are different from lapses in point of view and from shifting or multiple points of view, you will have to read experimental fiction. Some of the French writers who write the so-called "new novels" often experiment with point of view. In Alain Robbe-Grillet's novel *Jealousy*, for example, he makes his unlimited point of view ambiguous. In unlimited point of view, the author tells the reader how to interpret the characters' behavior or the novel's action. In an ambiguous unlimited point of view, the author presents all the possible interpretations for the characters' behavior or the novel's action without telling the reader which to choose. Here is an example from *Jealousy*:

> The main character . . . is a customs official. [He] is not an official but a high ranking employee of an old commercial company. This company's business is going badly. . . . [Its] business is going extremely well. The chief character . . . is dishonest. He is honest; he is trying to reestablish the situation compromised by his predecessor, who died in an automobile accident. . . . It was not an accident.

Robbe-Grillet does the same thing in his novel *In the Labyrinth*. In the novel, a soldier who's trying to deliver a package for a dead comrade becomes lost in a maze of streets in an unfamiliar village. The novel is written in such a way that the reader becomes metaphorically lost in the labyrinth of the novel; it's often unclear whether the soldier is actually in various places, such as the bar, or in a painting of the bar.

The novel begins with first-person point of view, switches in the next sentence to second person, then in the next paragraph to unlimited point of view. The novel doesn't return to first person until the last few pages, then to second person in the last paragraph and finally to first person in the last sentence. Though the majority of the novel is written in unlimited point of view, it often becomes quite ambiguous as Robbe-Grillet gives the reader multiple possibilities of interpretation.

> In his present position, the lame man is standing in his way. The soldier would have to shove him aside in order to step off the stairs and reach the door to the street. The soldier wonders if this is the same person as the man he met in the apartment of a woman with pale eyes. The man, as a matter of fact, who told him of the existence of this pseudo-barracks for invalids. If it's not the same man, why should he speak to the soldier as if he knew him? If it is the same man, how did he get here on his crutch through the snow-covered streets? And why?

Because Robbe-Grillet does not tell us how to interpret the actions in this scene and does not provide answers to his questions, the unlimited point of view becomes ambiguous. This author-as-God may, in fact, know all the answers, but he doesn't tell his readers which answer is the correct one.

The third part of my first novel, *The Kommandant's Mistress*, written in unlimited point of view, is also ambiguous but only when read after the first two parts of the novel. Read in isolation, this section of the novel, which purports to be the biographical encyclopedia entries of the novel's protagonists, does not seem ambiguous. However, when read in conjunction with the first two parts of the novel, it is clear that the fictional biographer has made some mistakes and errors of interpretation concerning the protagonists' lives. Because the reader is already familiar with the narratives told by the Kommandant and by the Jewish inmate he forces to become his mistress, these inconsistencies make the unlimited point of view of the third section of the novel highly ambiguous.

(See chapter 1 for an example of this from my novel, under the section titled "Different Points of View.")

One way to make unlimited point of view ambiguous is to present multiple interpretations of the same event—a character's emotional state, for example—so that the readers will be forced to interpret it themselves. "The woman looked annoyed, or angry, or pensive, or bitter, or merely sad" is an example of ambiguous unlimited point of view because the author does not tell the readers which emotion she wants the readers to choose for the character.

Qualifying your writing with words like "seems," "appears," "apparently," "probably," "perhaps," "may," etc.; providing multiple interpretations for the novel's actions without indicating which is the correct or best one; and posing unanswered questions will all make unlimited point of view ambiguous.

FINAL WORDS ON UNLIMITED POINT OF VIEW

For an author, unlimited point of view is, without a doubt, the easiest point of view in which to write novels. There are no restrictions or limitations on the type of information you can present to the readers. You can move freely from character to character; you can reveal information that is either inside or outside their heads; you can reveal any motivations, thoughts or feelings that you wish, whether or not these things are expressed aloud. You can also offer multiple interpretations for your novel's actions, without guiding the readers toward choosing only one, making the unlimited point of view ambiguous.

TIP Use unlimited point of view if you want total and complete freedom in terms of the information you present to your readers.

EXERCISES FOR UNLIMITED POINT OF VIEW

1. Write a scene involving at least three characters having a conflict. Even if you include dialogue in the scene, show the thoughts, feelings and unspoken motivations of all three characters. Present everything about one character before moving on to the next char-

acter. Each of the characters should be presented equally sympathetically, that is, your readers should understand the motivations and behavior of all three characters equally. If you can, try to make your readers feel the same level of emotion about each of the three characters. Pay attention to your word choice—especially your choice of verbs, adverbs and adjectives—as a way of controlling your readers' interpretation of the characters and their behavior. Show the scene to your readers for their feedback and suggestions for improvement.

2. Do exercise 1 again, only this time present the information about the characters in a more flexible manner, that is, go back and forth among the characters so that the information on any one character is not presented all at the same time, in the same paragraph. Each of the characters should be presented equally sympathetically. Show the scene to your readers for their feedback and suggestions for improvement.

3. Write a stream-of-consciousness passage in unlimited point of view from the perspective of only one character. Show the character's thoughts, feelings, memories, sensory impressions, etc., in a continuous, associative "stream." Show the scene to your readers for their feedback and suggestions for improvement.

4. Write a stream-of-consciousness passage in unlimited point of view from the perspective of several characters. Show the thoughts, feelings, memories, sensory impressions, etc., of each of the characters in continuous, associative "streams." Show the scene to your readers for their feedback and suggestions for improvement.

5. Write a scene in unlimited point of view from the perspective of an animal or which focuses on an animal. If you are not familiar with the animal you've chosen, then watch some of the animal shows on PBS, Discovery Channel or Animal Planet. The goal in this exercise is not to personify the animal, that is, you do not want to give it human characteristics. For example, don't write a scene in which an animal is unhappy because his wife left him and wants a divorce. Even though you are writing this scene in unlimited point of view, you need to think like the animal, see the world as the animal does, feel as the animal does. Read Jack London's *The Call of the Wild* and *White Fang* if you need help getting started.

Show the conflict (between animals, animal and people, animal and setting, etc.), the history of the relationship between (or among) the animals or people in the scene, and the nature of the characters involved. Make sure your readers understand the animal's actions, behavior and motivations, even if they don't approve of them. Show the scene to your readers for their feedback and suggestions for improvement.

6. Write a scene in unlimited point of view from the perspective of an inanimate object without personifying it. Even though you are writing this scene in unlimited point of view, you need to think like the object, see the world as the object does, feel as the object does. Show the scene to your readers for their feedback and suggestions for improvement.

7. Write a scene in ambiguous unlimited point of view. That is, you are godlike in that you know all the possible reasons for your character's actions, but you do not choose to tell the readers only one reason: Instead, you present all the reasons. That means you must present multiple interpretations of the character's behavior and the scene's action or qualify your writing so there is more than one way of viewing the scene, posing unanswered questions, etc. Show the scene to your readers for their feedback and suggestions for improvement.

8. Pick any novel written in unlimited point of view (many are mentioned in this chapter and in the appendices) and try to determine which passages indicate the author's moral judgment of the characters or the characters' inner lives.

THREE

FIRST-PERSON POINT OF VIEW

Point of view controls the reader's impression of everything else.
ROBERT SCHOLES AND ROBERT KELLOGG,
QUOTED BY SUSAN SNIADER LANSER
The Narrative Act: Point of View in Prose Fiction

First-person point of view is one of the easier and also one of the more challenging points of view. It's easier than outer limited, for example, because it allows you and your readers direct access to the narrator's thoughts, feelings and motivations. It's more intimate than unlimited because the reader experiences the world only through your narrator, creating an empathetic bond that is more difficult to achieve in unlimited or outer limited points of view.

First-person point of view is more challenging because of its limitations. In this point of view, you are restricted to viewing the world the way your narrator views it. The greatest danger to an inexperienced writer using first person is her unconsciously slipping into unlimited point of view (see chapter 10 for examples).

FIRST-PERSON POINT OF VIEW

First-person point of view has an "I" or "we" telling the story, and the character telling the story is the narrator. Since we are inside the narrator's head, all her thoughts, feelings and motivations are revealed. The thoughts, feelings and motivations of other characters are not revealed to the readers unless they are explicitly stated to the narrator (or in her vicinity so that she can overhear them). The narrator can judge the other characters, but the author does not openly present her own personal judgments.

Why First-Person Point of View Is Always Limited

First person is always a limited point of view because the readers see the world from within the head of the character who is narrating the story. If the author goes outside the narrator's head, for example, presenting information in another character's head, then the author is no longer in first-person (but, instead, in unlimited) point of view.

ADVANTAGES OF USING FIRST-PERSON POINT OF VIEW

Because you present the story from within the narrator's head, it is easier for your readers to develop an emotional attachment to the narrator. After all, they only get the story from her perspective. This is one of the easiest ways to create sympathy for unsympathetic characters. You can also establish a distinct voice for your narrator (more about voice in chapter 10). Though the story is limited to the narrator's perspective, the emotional bond between the protagonist and the readers is stronger in first-person than in any other point of view.

Twentieth-century literary fiction, as a genre, extensively uses first-person point of view, perhaps because it allows the author to explore the psychological idiosyncrasies of the narrators (and, by implication, of human beings in general). Mystery, detective and noir fiction also use first-person point of view regularly; other genres of commercial fiction, such as romance and science fiction, however, rarely employ this point of view, so you need to take your genre into consideration as an author when deciding which point of view is right for your novel.

DISADVANTAGES OF USING FIRST-PERSON POINT OF VIEW

As I explained under myth #9 in chapter 1, if you are honestly writing in first-person point of view, you cannot, as some authors believe, gradually fade into unlimited point of view by doing it in stages. If you are in one character's head, then you cannot get out of it without damaging the credibility of your point of view.

Therefore, once you have chosen first-person point of view, you are limited to presenting the information that the narrator himself can know or observe directly. This is often not an easy task, especially if you have something you want the reader to know that the narrator himself doesn't know. For example, if you are writing a novel in first-person point of view from the perspective of a wife whose husband is unfaithful, you might show her misinterpreting the unfamiliar shade of lipstick on her husband's collar or believing her husband's lies about it.

Maintaining reader sympathy or empathy for a character in denial is extremely challenging since the reader could begin to think the character is stupid. Working through challenges such as limiting the worldview to one character's perspective is one of the things that makes creative writing exciting, and I suspect that the writers who simply ignore these challenges are either unaware that they have switched point of view or simply do not care that they have.

FIRST-PERSON POINT OF VIEW
IN LITERARY FICTION

First-person point of view is extremely popular in literary fiction. Some authors write in it exclusively, and many literary authors use it in at least one book. Here's an excerpt from chapter 1 of Meg Files's novel *Meridian 144*:

> Only once before in my life have I ever recognized that I would have to die. I did not believe in my own death. Surely I would not die hugging the gun barrel of a World War II wreck.

And here's the opening from Stephen Dobyns's *The Church of Dead Girls*:

> This is how they looked: three dead girls propped up in three straight chairs. . . . I didn't witness this. I only looked at the photographs my cousin showed me. There were many photographs. And he said the police had a videotape of the entire attic, but I never saw it.

There are many, many literary novels—both older and contemporary—written in first-person point of view. It would be impossible to name them all. And these novels have a wide range of narrators: male/female, young/old, sane/insane, reliable/unreliable, etc. Read literary fiction, and you'll find novels written in first-person point of view.

FIRST-PERSON POINT OF VIEW IN COMMERCIAL FICTION

Despite the myth that commercial fiction is always written in unlimited point of view (see myth #1 in chapter 1), there is a great deal of commercial fiction written in first person. Peter Straub's *Mr. X* provides alternating first-person narratives, and Stephen King's *Dolores Claiborne* is written in first-person point of view. Many detective novels are narrated by their protagonists. Here's an excerpt from the first chapter of Mickey Spillane's *The Body Lovers*:

> I heard the screams through the thin mist of night and kicked the car to a stop at the curb. . . . I grabbed the flashlight from the glove compartment and climbed out, picked a path through the mounds of refuse and ran into the shadows, getting closer to frenzied shrieks, not knowing what to expect. Anything could have happened there.

Despite the proliferation of commercial novels written in unlimited point of view, there is also a tremendous number of commercial novels written in first person, including science fiction, like Jules Verne's *A Journey to the Center of the Earth*, and romances, like Barbara Hazard's *The Wary Widow*.

WHAT'S THE DIFFERENCE BETWEEN AUTHOR, PERSONA AND NARRATOR?

Many readers mistakenly assume that an "I" in the novel is the author. Even when the narrator is a clearly delineated character of a different age, race and gender than the author, readers and critics sometimes confuse the "I" of the novel with the author. The author is the person who actually wrote the book; the "I," on the other hand, is either a persona ("mask") or a narrator.

PERSONA

Sometimes the author adopts a persona, or mask, and from behind this mask, she comments in first-person point of view on the novel itself, on characters' behavior or on the world at large. The persona, which some critics call the "implied author," is not an actual character in the novel and is often unnamed; rather, she is simply a mouthpiece for certain political, sociological or other agendas that the author wishes to include in her work. Since the persona is not an actual character in the novel, she does not interact with the other characters. Here is an example from Fielding's *Tom Jones*, where the persona enters the work so often he has been called "intrusive" because of his interruptions (from book 1, chapter 5):

> As this is one of those deep observations which very few readers can be supposed capable of making themselves, I have thought proper to lend them my assistance; but this is a favor rarely to be expected in the course of my work. Indeed, I shall seldom or never so indulge him, unless in such instances as this, where nothing but the inspiration with which we writers are gifted can possibly enable any one to make the discovery.

A persona in the novel may not have the same beliefs as the author herself, so it is best not to assume that the persona is the author.

Why All the Confusion Between Author and Persona?
Sometimes an author gives the persona a life of his own. At other times, the elements of the persona's life correspond or are similar to events in the author's life. In Nathaniel Hawthorne's *The Scarlet Letter*, the persona claims to have worked in a customhouse, a job that Hawthorne himself worked for a period, and to have discovered the discarded, elaborately embroidered "A" worn by Hester Prynne. When elements of the author's and the persona's lives correspond, there can be confusion about whether the "I" in the novel is the author or a persona that he has adopted.

If the beliefs of the "I" in a novel match those of the author absolutely and unerringly, then the "I" can be considered to be the author's voice. Of course, the only way to determine whether the "I" is the author or the author's persona is to read everything the author has written—including nonfiction such as diaries, letters and essays—to see if the opinions expressed by the "I" in the novel are the same as those expressed by the author in his nonfiction work. If these beliefs do not match the author's, then it is assumed that the author has adopted a persona for the purposes of commenting on the work as he is writing it.

Intrusive Author/Persona

Eighteenth- and nineteenth-century novel readers simply assumed that the "I" who intruded into the story in order to comment on it was the author. Readers assumed, rightly or wrongly, that the novels were narrated by the authors themselves. Though the authors' personal beliefs may have, in fact, often corresponded with those of these intrusive personae, these stories were not necessarily narrated by the authors.

Do Intrusive Authors/Personae Work?

Do the intrusive personae of *Tom Jones*, *Middlemarch*, etc., work in an artistic sense? For some readers, these personae do; for others, they do not. This is a matter of taste and not a matter of correct or incorrect use of point of view. Though the trend in modern and contemporary literature is away from obviously intrusive authors or personae, it is still possible to employ that technique. Tom Robbins does it in chapter 100 of his novel *Even Cowgirls Get the Blues*.

> Well, here we are at Chapter 100. This calls for little celebration. I'm an author and therefore in the same business God is: If I say this page is a bottle of champagne, it's a bottle of champagne. Reader, will you share a cup of the bubbly with me? You prefer French to domestic? OK, I'll make it French. Cheers!

This section from the Robbins novel also includes second-person point of view, in which he directly addresses the reader (there's more on this in chapter 5).

Postmodernists often parody the eighteenth-century technique of an intrusive author/persona, having extremely intrusive personae come in to comment on their novels, such as the persona named Fowles does in John Fowles's *The French Lieutenant's Woman* (from chapter 61).

> It is a time-proven rule of the novelist's craft never to introduce any but very minor new characters at the end of the book . . . but the extremely important looking person that has, during the last scene, been leaning against the parapet of the embankment across the way from 16 Cheyne Walk . . . may seem at first sight to represent a gross breach of the rule. I did not want to introduce him; but since he is the sort of man who cannot bear to be left out of the limelight, . . . and since I am the kind of man who refuses to intervene in nature (even the worst), he has got himself in—or as he would put it, has got himself in *as he really is.*

The intrusive persona comes into the novel to make commentary about novel writing, interrupting the story at some of its most interesting parts.

Self-conscious, self-reflexive or disruptive narrators can also be found in Vladimir Nabokov's *Pale Fire* and *Lolita*, Doris Lessing's *The Golden Notebook*, Thomas Pynchon's *V*, John Barth's *Lost in the Funhouse*, Laurence Sterne's *Tristram Shandy* and J.D. Salinger's *The Catcher in the Rye*. Other postmodern authors whose work often includes such narrators are Kurt Vonnegut, Jorge Luis Borges, Walter Abish, Donald Barthelme, Robert Coover and Ishmael Reed.

Caution

Intrusive or disruptive personae can create emotional distance between the novel and its readers because the personae constantly remind readers that they are reading novels created by authors. Furthermore, as disruptive personae often interrupt the story just at its most interesting parts, the readers may become frustrated, if not angry, with the author. Many of the postmodernists use these disruptive personae precisely for that reason—to remind readers that they are merely powerless readers and that the author is in complete control of the fictional world they are entering. As with any other experiments in point of view, disruptive personae should be used sparingly and with extremely good reason.

If You Want to Use a Persona

If you wish to comment on your novel in the novel itself and you do not want a character or narrator making these comments, then you will be adopting a persona to make this commentary. The persona you create for your novel does not have to have the same beliefs that you do, and it will be up to you whether this persona has a distinct life of his own. Bear in mind that other characters in the novel should not interact with your persona since a persona is more of an implied character (see more about implied characters in chapter 12). You will use first-person point of view when your persona makes commentary in the novel.

TIP If you want to make comments about life, society, politics, etc., in your novel but don't want your readers to mistake these opinions for your characters', then use a persona. In a historical novel set during the French Revolution, for example, a character would be unable to make commentary on contemporary twentieth- or twenty-first–century politics since he would have died long before. A persona, however, because he is not a character in the novel, could draw parallels or make observations about the two distant time periods.

An intrusive author/persona should be interesting in his own right; in other words, the persona you adopt should be so interesting that, in effect, the persona becomes an implied character in the work. If skillfully written and presented, the commentary of this persona should add depth and complexity to the novel. Readers should look forward to this commentary, much as they might look forward to the conversations of their favorite dinner companions. When the readers look forward to these "intrusions" and find them interesting, valuable and worthwhile, then they are not intrusions at all, but simply pauses from the plot. In this situation, the intrusions work. They are not then intrusions in the strictest sense of the word (or in the way critics originally intended) but become character development for the implied character as well as a type of symbolic framework for the story being told.

TIP Read postmodernist and experimental fiction if you want to use your persona to make comments about writing in general and about your novel in particular, as well as about life, society, politics, etc., in your novel. Also, read the postmodernists if you want to parody the use of personae.

Final Words on Author and Persona

To state it simply, the author is the human being who creates the novel. The persona is a mask the author adopts in order to make commentary on the work or on the world; a persona is not an actual character in the novel that the other characters can interact with, but a persona may be an implied character.

NARRATORS

The narrator is an actual character in the work who is telling the story, a character that the other characters can see, hear and interact with. The narrator is neither the author nor the author's persona; he is a realistic character with his own life, emotions and beliefs. He can be an observer of or a participant in the story he's telling.

Sometimes, the author gives this narrator the same name as the author himself, but this narrator is not to be confused with the author. Chaucer did this in *The Canterbury Tales* when he named one of the characters Chaucer. Pilgrims are on a pilgrimage to the shrine of St. Thomas à Beckett and decide to have a storytelling contest. Chaucer the pilgrim introduces the reader to all the pilgrims in the general prologue, but Chaucer the pilgrim does not have the same beliefs as Chaucer the author, as this passage demonstrates:

> There was also a nun, a prioress,
> Whose smile was unaffected and demure;
> Her greatest oath was just, "By St. Eloi!"
> And she was known as Madame Eglantine.
> She sang the divine service prettily,
> And through the nose, becomingly intoned;
> And she spoke French well and elegantly

As she'd been taught it at Stratford-at-Bow,
For French of Paris was to her unknown . . .
Her cloak, I noticed, was most elegant.
A coral rosary with gauds of green [large beads that divided
smaller prayer beads into groups of ten]
She carried on her arm; and from it hung
A brooch of shining gold; inscribed thereon
Was, first of all, a crowned "A",
And under, *Amor vincit omnia* [Love conquers all].

Chaucer the pilgrim, who has probably never heard any language except English, admires the way she speaks French; Chaucer the author lets us know that she doesn't even speak "French of Paris" since she's learned French at Stratford-at-Bow, that is, she's learned it in England. The pilgrim recounts her behavior and clothing in great detail, admiring her coral rosary and her gold jewelry. Chaucer the author is letting us know that the Prioress is a nun who is obviously not very devout, being more devoted to worldly pleasures than to spiritual ones. Her rosary, which is for praying, is made of expensive coral beads, and her gold brooch, which a nun shouldn't even be wearing, has an extremely inappropriate and secular motto. It is clear that Chaucer the author is condemning her for her worldliness even while Chaucer the pilgrim is admiring her.

The narrator here, though he is given the same name as the author himself, does not share the same beliefs as the author. The narrator is not the author. Of course, Chaucer the author could have named his narrator pilgrim something different and had much the same effect, but Chaucer the author had a sense of humor: When Chaucer the pilgrim gets his turn to tell a story, he tells a story so boring that the other pilgrims won't let him finish it. So naming this pilgrim after himself is part of the humor in *The Canterbury Tales*.

Sometimes the narrator may not be actively participating in the main story he is relating; such a narrator is an observer rather than a participant in the story. Nick Carraway in Fitzgerald's *The Great Gatsby* narrates the story of Jay Gatsby. Nick is still actually present in the story—he and Gatsby have a relationship—but the main story is about Gatsby. The same is true of Jim Burden in Willa Cather's *My Ántonia*. It is Jim who tells us the life story of the immigrant Ántonia, though he rarely saw her after their childhood together. The narrator does not have to be telling the story about himself, but he does have to be a character in the novel itself, with whom other characters can interact, in order to be considered a narrator rather than a persona.

Reliable and Unreliable Narrators

Critic Wayne C. Booth, in his book *The Rhetoric of Fiction*, first used the terms *reliable* and *unreliable* to describe narrators. Booth defined a reliable narrator as a narrator whose beliefs and values reflect those of the author. Conventional use, however, defines a reliable narrator as one whose story can be judged as reliable and true. An unreliable narrator, on the other hand, is a narrator who is lying or who is unaware of the implications of the story he is relating, who is thus unreliable in this storytelling. To create a reliable narrator, therefore, you need simply have a narrator who is always reliable and trustworthy in the events and details he narrates.

Unreliable narrators, of course, may be lying, such as the Underground Man from Dostoevsky's *Notes from the Underground*. But there are many other reasons for a narrator to be unreliable. The narrator may be psychologically or emotionally impaired, such as in William Faulkner's novel *The Sound and the Fury*, where Benjy, who narrates part 1, is unreliable because he is retarded; his brother Quentin, the narrator of part 2, is unreliable because he's about to commit suicide and is therefore emotionally unstable. Narrators may be unreliable because they are naïve, manipulative, intoxicated, in denial, etc. In every case, except when the narrator is consciously lying, you should keep in mind that the narrators are telling the truth as they see it.

How to Create Unreliable Narrators

One of the greatest challenges in presenting unreliable narrators is determining how to present information to the reader that the narrator does not wish or is unable to reveal. It is imperative that authors understand psychology and human behavior in order to master point of view and create realistic, believable human characters. This is even more true when creating unreliable narrators who are not lying. It's relatively simple to create unreliable narrators who lie: You simply show them lying. Fyodor Dostoevsky's Underground Man in *Notes from the Underground* and Günter Grass's narrator in *Dog Years* both tell the reader that they've been lying about various parts of their stories.

It's much more challenging to create unreliable narrators who are not lying, who are, in fact, telling the truth as they see it. In his book *Vital Lies, Simple Truths: The Psychology of Self-Deception*, Daniel Goleman lists some of the most common psychological defenses that might make a person unreliable and that you can use to create unreliable narrators.

- **Repression:** forgetting and forgetting that one has forgotten; such as incest victims repressing their memories but not realizing they've forgotten anything
- **Denial and reversal:** a refusal to accept things as they are and transforming the denied fact into its opposite; thus "I hate you" becomes "I love you"
- **Projection:** acting as if one's own feelings or behavior are someone else's feelings/behavior; thus the unfaithful spouse accuses the faithful partner of infidelity
- **Isolation:** experiencing events without feelings; the unpleasant event is recalled but the associated feelings are not
- **Rationalization:** denial of one's true motives by covering over unpleasant impulses with a cloak of reasonableness; telling children that you're punishing them "for their own good," for example
- **Sublimation:** channeling instincts rather than repressing them; urges are acknowledged, but in a modified form; an impulse to steal becomes a career in banking, for instance
- **Selective inattention:** unsettling elements are edited from one's notice; misplacing unpleasant bills, for example
- **Automatism:** allowing entire sequences of behavior to go on without our having to notice them; for example, glancing at someone's genital area but not being aware of doing so

These are just a few psychological defense mechanisms that

you could give your character to cause your narrator to be unreliable. Even when the narrators are lying, however, bear in mind a quote from Daniel Goleman's *Vital Lies, Simple Truths:* "To lie well one must first believe one's own lies."

The more you familiarize yourself with human behavior and psychology, the easier it will be for you to create realistic characters including unreliable narrators. If you do decide to create an unreliable narrator, it will be important for you to learn how to reveal behavior that shows a narrator's unreliability so that the narrator doesn't have to say it. Other characters could notice something, but the narrator could not understand its significance or simply refuse to believe it. For example, your narrator may not believe his colleagues' warnings that he is about to be passed over for a promotion at work; later in the novel when the narrator does, indeed, lose the promotion, you have shown that the narrator is unreliable.

TIP Using first-person point of view for an unreliable or unsympathetic narrator is an extremely effective way to win your readers' emotional connection and get them to understand his behavior.

Final Words on Unreliable Narrators

Unreliable narrators are more common in literary fiction than in commercial fiction. When Agatha Christie first published *The Murder of Roger Ackroyd,* mystery readers were outraged to discover that the narrator, a kindly doctor, was the murderer because it is something of a convention in mysteries that the protagonist or narrator not be the criminal. Though the narrator had not actually lied in his narrative, he had neglected to tell us the rather important fact that he was the murderer.

Of course, all narrators may, ultimately, be unreliable because each character, like each human being, is only capable of telling his story from his own perspective. Furthermore, there is no absolute way of proving that a narrator is, indeed, reliable. Usually a narrator is judged reliable if nothing in the work itself contradicts his interpretation of events. These are philosophical dilemmas that most readers do not pursue. Whether or not you pursue these philosophical dilemmas as you write your own novel will be up to you.

STREAM-OF-CONSCIOUSNESS NARRATION

In stream-of-consciousness narration, you are attempting to render the thought processes of your characters, including memories and sense perceptions as well as thoughts. This can be done in first-person, inner limited or unlimited points of view. One of the most famous examples of this type of narration in first-person point of view comes from James Joyce's *Ulysses*. The final section of the book, which is in the head of Molly Bloom, the wife of the protagonist, just before she drifts off to sleep, contains her thoughts of her husband, Leopold, and of her lover, Blazes Boylan. In this passage Molly recalls having made love with Blazes that afternoon and having forced him to perform coitus interruptus so that she will not get pregnant.

I have quoted this passage at length so that you will get the full flavor of the way stream-of-consciousness passages work. Joyce originally wrote this passage without any punctuation or paragraphing whatsoever to indicate that the human mind does not use such mechanical devices in its thought processes. While I have not inserted periods or paragraphs, I have used apostrophes in contractions for your ease in reading.

> Yes when I lit the lamp yes because he must have come three or four times with that tremendous big red brute of a thing he has I thought the vein or whatever the dickens they call it was going to burst though his nose is not so big after I took off all my things with the blinds down after my hours dressing and perfuming and combing it like iron or some kind of thick crowbar standing all the time he must have eaten oysters I think a few dozen he was in great singing voice no I never in all my life felt anyone had one the size of that to make you feel full up he must have eaten a whole sheep after what's the idea making us like that with a big hole in the middle of us like a stallion driving it up into you because that's all they want out of you with that determined vicious look in his eye I had to half shut my

eyes still he hasn't such a tremendous amount of spunk in him when I made him pull it out and do it on me considering how big it is so much the better in case any of it wasn't washed out properly the last time I let him finish in me nice invention they made for women for him to get all the pleasure but if someone gave them a touch of it themselves they'd know what I went through with Milly

Molly's thoughts in this passage range from the actual sexual experience itself to her thoughts on the difference between men and women to her fears of another pregnancy.

Stream-of-consciousness passages do not have to be in first person (see chapter 2 for unlimited point of view stream of consciousness). Other works that include examples of stream-of-consciousness narrative in first person are William Faulkner's *The Sound and the Fury* and *As I Lay Dying* and my own novels *The Kommandant's Mistress* and *Only With the Heart*. Narrators are often considered to be speaking to someone other than themselves: other characters, the readers, etc. Stream-of-consciousness passages can allow you to reveal to the readers private thoughts that the narrator would never reveal to other characters in the book. You could also use these stream-of-consciousness passages to show partial memories, of child abuse, for example, that the narrator does not fully understand himself. Because stream of consciousness is solely within the narrator's mind and is not spoken aloud to other characters, you can explore the narrator's deepest psychological quirks and idiosyncrasies with it. If you wish to write such passages, read authors who are considered experts at stream-of-consciousness writing.

Interior Monologues

An interior monologue is a type of stream of consciousness in which the character's unspoken thoughts are revealed. Interior monologues are usually written in first-person point of view. The Molly Bloom passage on pages 48–49 is considered one of the finest examples.

FIRST-PERSON PLURAL POINT OF VIEW

If you're writing in first-person plural point of view, it means you do not have a single character narrating the story but rather a group of characters narrating the story, using the pronoun "we." If you decide to use first-person plural point of view, you must make sure that you fully develop the group consciousness behind the "we" so that the readers can determine the characteristics of the group narrating the story. That development means knowing the personalities and beliefs of the people who form the group.

When using first-person plural point of view, you do not need to know each character. Instead, you must know the entire group and its personality. Group members have common beliefs, attitudes and behavior that are intensified when they are together. Are your group members Christian fundamentalists awaiting Armageddon? Are they Nazis in South America evading prosecution for war crimes? Are they Vietnam veterans suffering from post-traumatic stress disorder? When using first-person plural point of view, you are concentrating on personality traits, beliefs and behavior that make your narrators members of a particular group rather than on those that make them unique individuals.

Walter Van Tilburg Clark's classic Western *The Ox-Bow Incident* occasionally employs first-person plural to show mob mentality. The narrator participates in a lynching, killing innocent men suspected of cattle rustling. When the author wishes to show the narrator succumbing to the mob mentality, the author switches from the "I" of first person to the "we" of first-person plural point of view. Because the narrator is no longer behaving as an individual but as part of the larger group—the lynch mob—and because the narrator is not acting from his own personal morals and beliefs in that scene, first-person plural point of view is more effective and is symbolic of the complex psychological process affecting him.

EPISTOLARY NARRATIVES

Epistolary novels are told through letters written by one or more of the characters, so they are a series of narratives written in first-person point of view. An advantage of a novel written in such a form is that letters give a sense of intimacy and immediacy. Epistolary narratives were extremely popular in the eighteenth century, and Samuel Richardson's *Pamela*, which contains both letters and a journal which is also addressed to her parents, was the first bestseller. It opens with a letter from Pamela:

> Dear Father and Mother: I have great trouble, and some comfort, to acquaint you with. The trouble is, that my good lady died of the illness I mentioned to you, and left us all much grieved for the loss of her; for she was a dear good lady, and kind to all us her servants. Much I feared, that as I was taken by her ladyship to wait upon her person, I should be quite destitute again, and forced to return to you and my poor mother, who have enough to do to maintain yourselves . . .

The letter contains urgency, which keeps the readers of the novel interested in continuing (see chapter 11 for further details); it gives us the social class and financial situation of Pamela and of her parents. It includes conflict by letting us see Pamela's worries about her situation in the household. The postscript of the letter adds even more urgency and conflict.

> I have been scared out of my senses; for just now, as I was folding up this letter in my late lady's dressing-room, in comes my young master!

This last section of the letter illustrates one of the disadvantages to epistolary novels: the idea of the character's writing a letter at the moment the upsetting event is happening. In fact, Henry Fielding parodied just this type of thing in his epistolary novel *Shamela*.

To Create Epistolary Novels

If you want to write an epistolary novel, you need to fully develop not only the letter writers but the letter recipients as well, whether or not they send any letters that end up in the novel. As with dialogue, the letters must show the characters' histories, natures and relationships (see more on dialogue in chapter 13); the letters should also fully develop your characters (see more on character development in chapter 12). Remember that letter writers have an audience—you need to make it clear who that intended audience is and develop it in the novel.

Of course, the novel need not be told entirely in letters. *Frankenstein* begins with letters but is not comprised entirely of letters. *Dracula* is a combination of letters, diary entries and ship's log entries; while *Gulliver's Travels* begins with a letter from Captain Gulliver to his Cousin Sympson, berating the cousin for convincing Gulliver to "publish a very loose and uncorrect account of my travels," which are in journal format. Alice Walker's *The Color Purple* is epistolary, E. Annie Proulx's *Postcards* combines postcards with narrative and Nick Bantock's famed *Griffin & Sabine* series is composed entirely of correspondence, including both letters and postcards. Even if you only include a section of letters in your novel, however, you should follow the guidelines for epistolary novels.

JOURNAL AND DIARY NARRATIVES

The first thing you have to decide if you're writing a novel in the form of a journal or a diary is whether the fictional author of this journal or diary—your character—expects to have an audience. Unlike letters, diaries are usually written for the private use of the diarist. It is rare that someone wishes to have his diary read by an outside reader. This is the most important thing to keep in mind if you have a character writing a private diary or a personal journal since these documents would be more psychologically revealing or intimate than those meant for an outside audience. For private diaries and journals, there is no audience, per se, unless it is the diarist himself at a later time in his life. This means that the diarist may be more honest and forthcoming about his emotions than he would be if he were writing a letter or directly addressing another character.

If your character is keeping a professional journal, however, such as a ship's log, then you would follow the same guidelines as for epistolary novels: Bear in mind who the journal is written for, and develop that audience fully.

The "discovered" diary or journal is a popular device. An adult child finds the diary of a deceased parent in Robert James Waller's

The Bridges of Madison County, and a bored man finds the journal of the adventurer Bowen Tyler in a quart thermos bottle off the coast of Greenland in Edgar Rice Burroughs's *The Land That Time Forgot.*

"Personal" diaries and journals are also an excellent way to reveal the voice of your narrator, as Nancy E. Turner did in *These Is My Words: The Diary of Sarah Agnes Prine, 1881–1901, Arizona Territories.* Here is an excerpt from the first chapter (the lack of apostrophes are the narrator's errors):

> A storm is rolling in, and that always makes me a little sad and wistful so I got it in my head to set to paper all these things that have got us this far on our way through this heathen land. Its been a sorrowful journey so far and hard and so if we dont get to San Angelo or even as far as Fort Hancock I am saving this little theme in my cigar box for some wandering travelers to find and know whose bones these is.

On the whole, writing a novel in the form of a diary or journal can give your readers insight into the fictional author of the diaries or journal. This form of narrative is often just as intimate as epistolary narratives.

E-MAIL, PHONE, INTERVIEW NARRATIVES, ETC.

If you want to write a high-tech version of an epistolary novel, with all the letters as e-mail, remember that most office e-mail is monitored by employers. That means if you write things that are too objectionable, the e-mail writer is likely to lose his job (or, at the very least, be disciplined). Of course, you could use that as part of your conflict. Personal e-mail accounts can also be monitored by the Internet service providers, so take that into account in your novel.

Phone call narratives would be like extended sections of dialogue, so all the guidelines for dialogue should be followed (see chapter 13 for more on dialogue). Nicholson Baker's *Vox* is told entirely as phone conversations, while Evelyn Waugh's *A Handful of Dust* has sections of phone calls.

Pretending that the novel is a series of taped conversations, taped monologues or a tape-recorded interview—all still presented in first-person point of view—is also popular. Scott Turow's legal thriller *Pleading Guilty* is presented as a series of tapes recorded by the novel's protagonist, Mack Malloy. The first page of the novel is presented as an office memorandum; the major parts of Turow's novel are titled "Tape 1, Tape 2," etc., and each tape has the date and time of its dictation indicated. Each part of the novel is then subdivided into other sections, which are individually titled "Your Investigator Gets Interrupted," "Your Investigator Visits Herbert Hoover's America," etc.

Anne Rice's classic *Interview With the Vampire* is set up as a taped interview, with the boy-interviewer occasionally interrupting the vampire's first-person monologues. Because Rice sets up her novel in unlimited point of view, written in the grammatical third person, but then has the bulk of the novel "spoken" or narrated by the vampire, she was forced to use quotation marks around the vampire's story (that is, every single paragraph of the vampire's tale has quotes around it), and she had to use single quotes within the vampire's tale to indicate dialogue.

There are many variations on these first-person narratives, and they can be used in conjunction with other points of view. Michael Crichton's industrial espionage thriller *Disclosure*, for example, is written primarily in unlimited point of view but makes extensive use of e-mail and office memorandum within the novel.

Thematic Benefits

Narratives that are written as phone calls give the illusion that they are even more intimate than the traditional first-person narratives since the setup implies a lack of authorial organization or intrusion. Taped conversations and taped monologues also imply a deeper, perhaps more intrusive intimacy; but as the author, you must take into account the implied audience of these tapes if you choose to use this device in your novel. Tape-recorded interviews have a stated audience, though the purpose of these interviews may be directly stated or only implied.

Of course, all of these devices—phone calls, tapes, interviews—may be used without a narrator, though this would be more challenging since it changes the point of view from first person to outer limited (see chapter 6).

AUTOBIOGRAPHICAL NARRATIVES

Narratives posing as the life story of the protagonist and written in first-person point of view are quite abundant. Sometimes, the author pretends to have found such a document, as Daniel Defoe did with his novel *Moll Flanders*. At other times, the narrator simply includes events and personages from his own life, as did James Joyce in *A Portrait of the Artist as a Young Man*, though Joyce's novel is written in inner limited point of view (see chapter 4 for an excerpt). The danger with this type of narrative is including every trivial life detail, which will slow down the narrative and bore the readers.

You can also parody first-person autobiographical narratives as J.D. Salinger did in his classic *The Catcher in the Rye*, which starts with this opening line:

> If you really want to hear about it, the first thing you'll probably want to know is where I was born, and what my lousy childhood was like, and how my parents were occupied and all before they had me, and all that David Copperfield kind of crap, but I don't feel like going into it, if you want to know the truth.

Many of the postmodernists parody other types of writing, including autobiographical novels; so if you're interested in writing parody, read experimental novelists and the postmodernists.

***

TIP First-person point of view creates the most intimate bond between the author, her readers and the novel's narrator.

***

FINAL WORDS ON FIRST-PERSON POINT OF VIEW

First-person point of view is one of the easier points of view in that it allows both the author and the readers immediate access to the narrator's thoughts, feelings and motivations, creating a strong emotional bond. If you can accept the challenges of restricting the novel's world view to that of the narrator, then this is an extremely interesting and exciting point of view.

EXERCISES FOR FIRST-PERSON POINT OF VIEW

1. If you do not have children or grandchildren of your own, visit a daycare center or a preschool for several days in a row. Observe the children: What's important to them? What do they care about? How do they express themselves? For this exercise, it is extremely important to observe several children of the same age, preferably interacting with each other as well as with adults. If you only observe one child, that child may not be representative of other children that age. Now write a paragraph in first-person point of view from the perspective of a five-year-old child having a conflict with a parent. Use vocabulary, sentence structure and images appropriate for a five-year-old. Show the conflict, the history of the relationship between (or among) the people in the scene and the nature of the characters involved. Someone reading this should know that this is a five-year-old without your telling him. Have someone who is very familiar with children read the scene and critique it. Are there any words not appropriate to a five-year-old? Do any of the sentences strike the reader as being inappropriate for a child of that age? Can the reader guess the age of the child without your telling him?

2. Write the same scene again in first-person point of view from the parent's perspective. Make sure the reader understands the narrator's actions, behavior and motivations, even if the reader doesn't approve of them. Show the conflict, the history of the relationship between (or among) the people in the scene and the nature of the characters involved. Have a parent of young children analyze the scene to determine if it is, indeed, the way a parent in that situation would think, react and respond.

3. Write the same scene again in first-person point of view from the perspective of a child (or parent) not directly involved in the conflict. How does this narrator feel about the conflict? How is she affected? How does she respond? Make sure that each of the perspectives in the first three exercises is significantly different from the other perspectives. The goal of these exercises is to really portray how each individual character is thinking, feeling and re-

acting. Though each is written in first-person point of view, they should not be identical. It should be clear to your readers that each narrator has a different personality and a different stake in the conflict. Show all three scenes to your readers for their feedback and suggestions for improvement.

4. Write a scene (one paragraph to one page in length) in which a man and a woman are having a conflict. Write the scene in first-person point of view from the man's perspective. Show the conflict, the history of the relationship between (or among) the people in the scene and the nature of the characters involved. If you are a woman, have several men read the scene to determine if you have accurately portrayed a man's perspective. (Even if you're a man, it wouldn't hurt to get other men's feedback on your male narrator.) This feedback is extremely important since a woman often thinks she's accurately portraying a man's perspective, but men would seriously disagree with her portrayal. Make sure your male readers analyze word choice, sentence structure, imagery, etc. If they say a man wouldn't use a certain word, ask which word a man would use. Trust your male readers to know what men think. Use their feedback to better learn to write in first-person point of view from a male perspective.

5. Write the scene from exercise 4 again, in first-person point of view, only this time from the woman's perspective. Show the conflict, the history of the relationship between (or among) the people in the scene and the nature of the characters involved. Make sure the readers understand the narrator's actions, behavior and motivations, even if the readers don't approve of them. Have your readers follow the same guidelines in exercise 4. Use their feedback to better learn to write in first-person point of view from a female perspective.

6. Read several of the following novels, all of which are written in first-person point of view and which have unreliable narrators.

Fyodor Dostoevsky's *Notes from the Underground*
William Faulkner's *The Sound and the Fury*
Kaye Gibbons's *Ellen Foster*
Patrick McCabe's *The Butcher Boy*
Patrick McGrath's *Asylum*
Patrick McGrath's *The Grotesque*

Patrick McGrath's *Spider*
Sherri Szeman's *The Kommandant's Mistress*
Sherri Szeman's *Only With the Heart*
Mark Twain's *The Adventures of Huckleberry Finn*

Notice how these authors have handled unreliable narrators. Some are unreliable because they are children, some because they're liars, some because they're mentally unstable, some because they're in denial about their own motivations (hence, these narrators aren't consciously lying). Notice how the authors maintain their narrators' integrity while giving information to the readers of which the narrators may not be aware.

7. After you do exercise 6 or otherwise familiarize yourself with various types of unreliable narrators, write a scene in first-person point of view from the perspective of an unreliable narrator. Show the conflict, the history of the relationship between (or among) the people in the scene and the nature of the characters involved. Make sure the readers understand the narrator's actions, behavior and motivations, even if the readers don't approve of them. Show the scene to your readers, and ask them to determine whether or not the narrator is reliable, that is, can the reader trust absolutely everything that the narrator is saying? Have your readers point out passages that are suspect. If your readers indicate the passages where your narrator is, indeed, being unreliable, then you have succeeded. Now you have to determine whether the readers understand why your narrator has behaved the way he has.

8. Write a scene, in first-person point of view, as if it were a letter from any character's perspective. Since this is a letter, it is understood that the narrator writing the letter will have an audience. Who is her audience? What is the relationship between the writer and recipient of the letter? If the conflict is not between the writer and the recipient, then what is the writer's purpose for writing the letter? Show the conflict, the history of the relationship between (or among) the people in the scene and the nature of the characters involved. Make sure also that your readers understand the relationship between the letter writer and recipient.

9. Write a scene as if it were a diary or journal entry, in first-person point of view, from any character's perspective. Show the conflict, the history of the relationship between (or among) the

people in the scene and the nature of the characters involved. Show the scene to your readers for their feedback and suggestions for improvement.

10. Write a scene in first-person point of view from the perspective of an animal. If you are not familiar with animals, then watch some of the animal shows on PBS, Discovery Channel or Animal Planet. The goal in this exercise is not to personify the animal, that is, you do not want to give it human characteristics (at least, not beyond the ability to think cognitively in a way that we human readers can understand). So don't write a scene in which an animal is unhappy because his face broke out before a big date. To write this scene well, you need to become the animal. You have to think like the animal, see the world as the animal does, feel as the animal does. Read Jack London's *The Call of the Wild* and *White Fang* if you need help getting started. Show the scene to your readers for their feedback and suggestions for improvement.

11. Write a scene in first-person point of view from the perspective of an inanimate object (as you did for an animal in exercise 10). Show the scene to your readers for their feedback and suggestions for improvement.

FOUR

INNER LIMITED POINT OF VIEW

> Point of view is the overworked, underpaid servant of novel-writing. It slaves in the kitchen making the host and hostess—character and plot—look good out in the dining room.
>
> DONNA LEVIN
> *Get That Novel Written!*

To put it most simply, inner limited point of view is the same as first person but is written in the grammatical third person. In other words, the author picks one character and pretends he is in that character's head, limiting the information presented to the inner life of that chosen character. The author reveals all the thoughts, feelings and motivations of that character, but writes about him in the grammatical third person, using he, she, it or they to refer to his character. The author reveals the inner life of that one character and limits his presentation of the other characters to their outer lives.

The author stays out of the heads of all other characters in the novel. He doesn't present any of their thoughts, feelings or unspoken motivations unless they are revealed in dialogue to, or in the presence of, the character from whose perspective he is telling the story. The author presents only the external, observable behavior of the other characters.

In this sense, inner limited point of view is exactly like first-person point of view. Therefore, to master inner limited point of view, you need to first master all of the elements of writing in first person.

FIRST PERSON VS. INNER LIMITED
If inner limited point of view is exactly like first person, only written in the grammatical third person, then why would an author use

inner limited rather than first? First person is the most intimate of all the points of view. It allows both the author and the readers to have immediate access to the narrator's thoughts and feelings, so the readers often feel they know the narrator as well as they know themselves. Inner limited point of view, because it is written in the grammatical third person though referring to the character whose thoughts and feelings are revealed, creates a greater emotional distance between the author and the character as well as between the character and the readers. Perhaps because first person requires the author and readers to view the world of the novel using the first-person pronoun of "I," the intimacy is greater.

Theoretically, it would seem that the effect should be the same with merely a change in pronouns. In practice, however, the effect is dramatically different. When working on my third novel, about two brothers who decide to hunt down a serial killer themselves, I had a scene from a victim's perspective, originally written in first-person point of view. The scene was relatively short, considering the fact that it is the only appearance of the character in the novel—the scene was only three pages long. When I decided to change the point of view to inner limited, I knew it would create some distance for the reader due to the change in pronoun. What I didn't realize was the far greater emotional distance it would create for me as the author. Though I had written the scene in first person and knew the victim intimately, I could literally feel the emotional distance growing as I rewrote the scene in inner limited point of view.

First-person point of view simply creates a greater intimacy and a stronger bond between author, narrator and readers than inner limited does. Some of the postmodernists, like James Joyce, may have intentionally chosen inner limited rather than first-person point of view because of the emotional distance inner limited creates: Symbolically, it mirrors the spiritual alienation present in the twentieth century. As an author, however, be aware of this potential for emotional distance when using inner limited point of view so that you can determine which point of view, first or inner limited, will be most effective for your novel.

In some genres that rarely use first-person point of view, for example, science fiction or romance, you may be able to effectively use inner limited rather than the traditional unlimited point of view. In this way, you could maintain the emotional distance the readers expect in that genre while exploring some of the psychological and emotional arenas available to first-person point of view.

INNER LIMITED POINT OF VIEW
IN LITERARY FICTION

Inner limited is an unusual point of view simply because most authors write in first person rather than in the grammatical third if they are going to limit their work in this way. One of the masters of inner limited point of view was James Joyce. The opening paragraphs of his novel *A Portrait of the Artist as a Young Man* present the world to us as the protagonist, Stephen, sees and hears it when he's a toddler.

> Once upon a time and a very good time it was there was a moocow coming down along the road and this moocow that was coming down along the road met a nicens little boy named baby tuckoo . . .
>
> His father told him that story: his father looked at him through a glass: he had a hairy face.
>
> He was baby tuckoo. The moocow came down the road where Betty Byrne lived.

Later, when Stephen goes away to boarding school, Joyce presents some of his concerns and thoughts (also from chapter 1). Again, using inner limited point of view, Joyce presents these thoughts as if he's in Stephen's head but writes in the grammatical third person.

> It pained him that he did not know well what politics meant and that he did not know where the universe ended. He felt small and weak. When would he be like the fellows in poetry and rhetoric?

Joyce continuously gives us Stephen's inner life but gives us only the outer, observable reactions of the other boys and of everyone else in the novel. Rather than writing in first-person point of view, using Stephen as a narrator, Joyce writes in the grammatical third person. The information given to the readers is virtually identical to that given in first-person point of view. The readers have access to all Stephen's thoughts, motivations and feelings, but the emotional distance between the readers and Stephen is greater because of the author's choice of point of view.

Henry James also uses inner limited point of view, limiting the information he gives his readers to the inner life of one character and to the outer lives of the others. Here's an example from part 1, chapter 1 of *The Ambassadors*:

> Strether's first question, when he reached the hotel, was about his friend; yet on his learning that Waymarsh was apparently not to arrive till evening he was not wholly disconcerted.

When an author limits her presentation of the novel's world from within one character's head but uses the grammatical third person, the author is using inner limited point of view—limiting our view of the novel's world to the inner life of one character and the outer lives of all the others.

Some postmodernist authors, like Margaret Drabble in her novel *The Waterfall* and Marguerite Duras in her novel *The Lover*, alternate between inner limited and first-person points of view to show the psychological state of mind of the narrator during certain times of his life, for example, when the narrator might be feeling emotionally distant from himself and his own behavior (see more on this in chapters 8 and 9).

INNER LIMITED POINT OF VIEW
IN COMMERCIAL FICTION

In commercial fiction, especially suspense and detective fiction, inner limited point of view is alternated with unlimited, with the inner limited point of view reserved for passages depicting the criminal's or the victim's perspective and unlimited point of view used for the protagonist crime-fighters' perspective. An explanation of this and examples can be found in chapter 7 on combo point of view.

FINAL WORDS ON INNER LIMITED POINT OF VIEW

So what are the advantages to inner limited point of view over first person? Emotional distance. Some authors and readers are simply more comfortable reading novels written in the grammatical third person. Some of the postmodernists may have chosen inner limited point of view as a metaphor for the sense of individual isolation and spiritual alienation prevalent after World War I. Some authors, like James Joyce and Marguerite Duras, may have wanted to include autobiographical information in their novels while pretending that such information was fictional.

In the case of commercial crime novels, the choice of inner limited point of view for the criminals clearly serves to keep the readers from becoming too emotionally involved or from feeling connected to the criminals. Too great an emotional connection with a fictional killer could be misconstrued as author sympathy for the criminals or, conversely, as a lack of consideration for the victims of such crime. (Authors of literary fiction, in fact, often use the intimacy of first person when portraying criminals in order to make the readers reevaluate their own responses to violence.)

Using inner limited for the victim allows the readers access to the victim's thoughts while protecting the readers from the emotional devastation they might feel when something happens to that character. First-person point of view would increase the readers' emotional bond and, thus, their distress when something bad happened to the character. Inner limited point of view, when used to write about a victim of crime, also allows the readers to re-create the crime, just as professional crime-fighters do (more on this specific use of inner limited point of view in commercial fiction in chapter 7).

When to Use Inner Limited Point of View

Use inner limited point of view instead of first person under these conditions:

- You want to limit your perspective to only one character's inner, psychological life while presenting only the exterior, outer lives of the other characters.
- You're more comfortable writing in the grammatical third person.
- You believe that your readers would be more comfortable reading the grammatical third person.
- You want to increase the emotional distance between you

and the character or between the character and the readers while maintaining access to a character's inner life.

- You want to increase the emotional distance between the character and the readers while still revealing that character's inner life.

TIP Using inner limited point of view for a killer allows you to access the killer's mind without the risk of too great an emotional involvement, either on your part or on that of your readers. Too great an emotional involvement may make your readers hostile to you since it may make them believe that you approve of violence or of the killings. This may be one reason inner limited point of view is used so frequently in the combo point of view in commercial suspense and mystery fiction.

EXERCISES FOR INNER LIMITED POINT OF VIEW

1. Do any of the exercises listed under first-person point of view, only write them in inner limited point of view, in the grammatical third person, using he, she, it or they. While you write, make sure you pay special attention to the increase or decrease in the emotional distance between you and the character. Which feels more comfortable to you, writing in first person or in inner limited? Why?

2. Write any scene in inner limited point of view. Show the conflict, the history of the relationship between (or among) the people in the scene and the nature of the characters involved. Make sure the readers understand the narrator's actions, behavior and motivations, even if the readers don't approve of them.

FIVE

SECOND-PERSON POINT OF VIEW

What is it about "you" that literary critics and
theorists find so embarrassing?

ROBYN R. WARHOL

Gendered Interventions: Narrative Discourse in the Victorian Novel

Dear readers, you've come to the really interesting part of the book. Yes, it's you being talked to, dear reader, the person actually reading this book, and since you're being directly addressed, using the grammatical second person, this sentence is written in second-person point of view. (Actually second-person point of view has been used throughout this book, dear reader, whenever you and your own novel have been discussed.) Second-person point of view directly addresses someone—not in dialogue—as "you." This directly addressed "you" may be the readers, as it is here and which it most frequently is in pretwentieth-century novels, it may be other characters in the novel, it may be other imaginary or real personages outside the novel, it may be humanity in general or it may be implied characters in the novel (see more on implied characters in chapter 12). Using second-person point of view calls attention to the fact that you're writing a novel, especially if you address your audience as "reader."

IS SECOND-PERSON POINT OF VIEW UNUSUAL?

Using second-person point of view periodically throughout a novel is not unusual. In fact, it is quite common and occurs far more frequently than literary critics would lead readers to believe. It is even present in nonfiction. For example, Ian Frazier, in his nonfiction book entitled *On the Rez*, about the Oglala Sioux on the Pine

Ridge Indian Reservation, does it frequently. Here is an example from chapter 11:

> Imagine that the hopeful, innocent, unbounded fantasy you had about someone you really admired when you were a child . . . [simply continued] to grow. . . .

Later on the same page, Frazier does it again, this time combining first and second person just as his counterparts in the eighteenth and nineteenth centuries did when they wrote their novels.

> Reader, books are long, and I know that even the faithful reader tires. But I hope a few of you are still with me here. As much as I have wanted to tell anything, I want to tell you about SuAnne.

So second-person point of view appears quite frequently, both in novels and nonfiction, even in contemporary work. Most often second person is used in conjunction with first-person point of view. There are also quite a few contemporary short stories written entirely in second person. What is rare, however, is to have an entire novel written in second-person point of view.

ADVANTAGES OF SECOND-PERSON POINT OF VIEW

The advantages of using second-person point of view are that your audience may feel directly connected to you as the author and may feel more intimately involved with the characters and the action in the novel when directly addressed. Also, the author can make comments that connect the reader to all humanity using second person. The author can also make her other characters come more alive, especially narrators, by having them "speak" directly to someone but not in dialogue.

DISADVANTAGES OF SECOND-PERSON POINT OF VIEW

The disadvantage of using second-person point of view, especially if writing an entire novel in this style, is that as soon as your readers no longer feel that the "you" being addressed and described applies to them, you may lose the readers' interest in your work. Also, according to Robyn R. Warhol, author of *Gendered Interventions: Narrative Discourse in the Victorian Novel*, some twentieth-century critics find the second-person direct address "sensational," consider it to be lacking in "genuineness" or believe that such address "holds a strong implication of judgment, of moral or didactic aims." Also, as some critics complained about Jay McInerney's novel *Bright Lights, Big City*, written entirely in second person, this point of view may keep your audience at an emotional distance because it prevents them from identifying with the character, who is referred to as "you," which also can mean the reading audience.

Despite these ostensible disadvantages, however, second-person point of view still appears regularly in fiction, both literary and commercial.

SECOND-PERSON POINT OF VIEW IN LITERARY FICTION

The "you" of second-person point of view can refer to many different people. It can refer to the novel's readers, to other characters (actual or implied) in the novel, to humanity in general or to real persons outside the novel who are not the readers.

"You" as the Novel's Readers

One of the most famous usages of second-person point of view in all literature comes from Charlotte Brontë's novel *Jane Eyre*, in chapter 38, when the narrator, Jane, speaking of her reunion with her beloved Mr. Rochester, introduces second-person point of view into her first-person narrative by saying, "Reader, I married him." Later in that same chapter, speaking of Mr. Rochester's adopted daughter, Brontë writes, "You have not quite forgotten little Adèle, have you, reader?" Jane then goes on to tell us what happened to Adèle after Jane and Mr. Rochester got married.

In Vladimir Nabokov's *Lolita*, when the betrayed wife, Charlotte, orders her husband, the narrator, to leave the room, Nabokov writes, "Reader, I did" (part 1, chapter 22), addressing the reading audience. When the narrator, Humbert Humbert, is discussing his fantasies of murdering his wife, he says, "Simple, was it not? But what d'ye know, folks—I just could not make myself do it" (part 1, chapter 20). Some critics have interpreted this line as Humbert's addressing the jury at his murder trial, but since he never addresses the jury in such a flippant manner anywhere else in the book, he is probably addressing the readers here.

"You" as Other Actual Characters in the Novel

The "you" addressed in second-person point of view does not always have to be the author's reading audience. The "you" can be other characters—actual or implied—in the novel. At times, the "you" being addressed is another character. Nabokov does this in *Lolita*, when the narrator addresses his love interest, his stepdaughter Lolita (from part 2, chapter 10):

> I would . . . forget all my masculine pride and literally crawl on my knees to your chair, my Lolita! You would give me one look . . . "Oh no, not again . . . Pulease, leave me alone, will you," you would say, "for Christ's sake leave me alone."

Most often in this novel, however, Nabokov uses second-person point of view when the narrator, who is accused of murder, is addressing the jury, who are only implied characters in the novel because they never actually appear (more on this in the next section and in chapter 12). "Ladies and gentlemen of the jury—I wept" (part 1, chapter 17), and, after Humbert has recounted having had sex with Lolita for the first time, "Sensitive gentlewomen of the jury, I was not even her first lover" (part 1, chapter 23). So the "you" in second-person point of view can refer to other characters in the novel as well as to the novel's readers.

"You" as Implied Characters

Many times in novels written in first-person point of view, the narrator is aware of herself as storyteller and is highly conscious of her audience, whether it be her readers or other actual characters in the novel, as many of the examples in the previous section indicate. At other times, however, though the narrator does not mention her audience by name, it is still clear that the narrator is speaking specifically to someone. When a narrator does this, she is speaking to an implied audience or an implied character. For example, when Max, the Kommandant in my first novel is telling his story, he often seems to be talking to someone. He says things like, "It's difficult to explain to someone who wasn't there." Later, when he's discussing the time he had to teach inexperienced SS men how to shoot prisoners, he suddenly begins telling his implied character/audience about something else entirely (from part 1, chapter 9).

> [My subordinate] hurried over to the prisoners and began shouting instructions. I pulled out a cigarette. A nasty habit, I know. I was always trying to quit. I did manage to quit smoking once I got to the camp. I was always so busy I didn't have the time for it. But I still smoked then. Sometimes nothing else would do.

Though he does not use the second-person address of "you," the Kommandant is clearly addressing his remarks to someone and is, furthermore, seeking the approval of this implied audience. Since the Kommandant himself was present at the event he is relating, it is obvious that he is making his remarks to someone else who was not at the scene when he says, "It's difficult to explain to someone who wasn't there." Whether the Kommandant is actually addressing the character or merely contemplating doing so, the addressed character is implied. The Kommandant is trying to distract his listener's attention away from the seriousness of the Nazis' shooting Jewish civilians and to focus the audience's attention onto the rather trivial offense of the Kommandant's smoking too many cigarettes.

At other times the Kommandant's narrative seems to be answering questions, ostensibly asked by the implied character, as when the Kommandant says, "No, I wasn't afraid. I wasn't strong enough," or "No, that wasn't running away. That was saving myself."

You can have your narrators, who are characters in the novels, address an implied audience by using second-person point of view. You can also make your readers implied characters in the novel, as do many postmodernists. John Hawkes does exactly this in *The Lime Twig*, when the "you" (the readers of the novel) is attributed with specific dramatic actions and shared experiences with the characters in the literature, thus making the readers implied characters in the text.

"You" as Humanity in General

The "you" of the second-person address can be a more nebulous, generalized audience, so that the "you" means all human beings. Nabokov does this in *Lolita*: "You can always count on a murderer for a fancy prose style" (part 1, chapter 1). Günter Grass also uses second-person point of view to address humanity in general in his novel *The Tin Drum* (from "The Wide Skirt" in book 1).

> You can begin a story in the middle and create confusion by striking out boldly, backward and forward. . . . Or you can declare at the very start that it's impossible to write a novel nowadays, but then, behind your own back so to speak, give birth to a whopper, a novel to end all novels.

SECOND-PERSON POINT OF VIEW IN POSTMODERNIST FICTION

Postmodernist fiction revels in using second-person point of view, most often to parody its use in previous centuries. Tom Robbins, in *Even Cowgirls Get the Blues*, addresses the readers and makes them implied characters in chapter 100.

> Reader, will you share a cup of the bubbly with me? You prefer French to domestic? OK, I'll make it French. Cheers!

(The full paragraph from which this excerpt is taken appears in chapter 3 of this book, under the section titled "Do Intrusive Authors/Personae Work?") In Robbins's book, the directly addressed readers begin to get a negative attitude when the author insists that his novels can teach them something.

> "For example?" you ask snottily, while helping yourself to my champagne . . . The author can sense that chapter 100 displeases you. Not only does it interrupt the story, it says too much and says it too didactically . . . Come on, now, that's enough champagne. Either give me a kiss or get out of here.

So Robbins annoys his readers by interrupting the story to tell them they *should* be annoyed by interruptions in the story and by an author's use of second-person address. This is a common technique in postmodernist fiction, parodying the very thing as it's being done. Then Robbins's audience, after drinking champagne with the author, even gets a chance to become intimate with him. The author performs this feat by using second-person point of view.

Donald Barthelme, in his novel *Snow White*, uses second-person point of view in a questionnaire in the middle of the novel, interrupting the storyline in typical postmodernist fashion.

1. Do you like the story so far? ☐ Yes ☐ No
2. Does Snow White resemble the Snow White you remember? ☐ Yes ☐ No
3. Have you understood, in reading to this point, that Paul is the prince-figure? ☐ Yes ☐ No
4. That Jane is the wicked stepmother-figure?
   ☐ Yes ☐ No
5. In the further development of the story, would you like
   ☐ more emotion or ☐ less emotion?

As is common in postmodernist fiction, Barthelme uses second-person point of view not only to directly address his audience, involving the audience in the work itself, but also to parody second-person point of view, as in later questions in this survey when he wanders into topics unrelated to the novel itself, such as this one.

12. Do you feel that the Authors Guild has been sufficiently vigorous in representing writers before the Congress in matters pertaining to copyright legislation? ☐ Yes ☐ No

Postmodernist authors do not limit themselves to one meaning of "you" when using second-person point of view. In Grass's *The Tin Drum*, the "you" refers to multiple readers, all at the same time: the readers of Oskar's manuscript, who are also the narrator's visitors, as well as the readers of Grass's novel.

I shall begin far away from me; for no one ought to tell the story of his life who hasn't the patience to say a word or two about at least half of his grandparents before plunging into his own existence. And so to you personally, dear reader, who are no doubt leading a muddled kind of life outside this institution, to you my friends and weekly visitors who suspect nothing of my paper supply, I introduce Oskar's maternal grandmother.

As you can see, there's no limit to the meanings that "you" can have when using second-person point of view in your novel. As long as you make it clear to your reader who it is that's being addressed when you use second person, you can use it whenever you like.

BUT AN ENTIRE NOVEL
IN SECOND-PERSON POINT OF VIEW?

Although it is certainly challenging to write an entire novel in second-person point of view, it is obviously possible, as Jay McInerney's *Bright Lights, Big City* demonstrates. The novel begins like this:

> You are not the kind of guy who would be at a place like this at this time of the morning. But here you are, and you cannot say that the terrain is entirely unfamiliar, although the details are fuzzy. You are at a nightclub talking to a girl with a shaved head. The club is either Heartbreak or the Lizard Lounge. All might come clear if you could just slip into the bathroom and do a little more Bolivian Marching Powder. Then again, it might not. A small voice inside you insists that this epidemic lack of clarity is a result of too much of that already. . . .

McInerney maintains second-person point of view throughout the entire novel, taking us through his protagonist's troubles with drugs, getting fired from his job and reliving his mother's agonizing death—all in second-person point of view.

This point of view could have created distance between the protagonist and the readers since the protagonist, who uses drugs and has an unpleasant personality, is identified by the pronoun "you" throughout, which could also be considered as addressing the readers of the novel. Despite this, McInerney manages to create a bond between his readers and his protagonist by fully developing the protagonist as a completely human character—one with flaws, it is true, but one who is approaching moral redemption and a change of lifestyle by the end of the novel. It is probably this moral redemption that prevents the readers from becoming outraged by their forced association with the protagonist through the second-person point of view.

In another point of view, the novel would not have been as shocking. It would have become just another story of an addict. The relatively jarring and unusual choice of second-person point of view throughout McInerney's entire novel, because it forced the readers to associate themselves with the protagonist, may have been the very thing that contributed to its success.

DISCUSSING YOUR AUDIENCE IN GRAMMATICAL THIRD PERSON

Henry Fielding, in his masterpiece *Tom Jones*, often directly addresses his audience using second-person point of view, as in this excerpt from book 4, chapter 2:

> Reader, perhaps thou hast seen the statue of the *Venus de Medicis*. . . . If thou hast seen [this] without knowing what beauty is, thou hast no eyes; if without feeling its power, thou hast no heart.

But Fielding also involves his readers by simply talking about them in the novel, using the grammatical third person—he, she, it and they—to refer to his readers as he does here (from book 1, chapter 25):

> But as we cannot possibly divine what complexion our reader may be, and as it will be some time before he will hear any more of Jenny, we think proper to give him a very early intimation, that Mr. Allworthy was, and will hereafter appear to be, absolutely innocent of any criminal intention whatever.

Notice that in this passage, Fielding is also reassuring his readers that everything will turn out well. Later, Fielding also claims to know his readers' emotions toward the novel's characters (from book 10, chapter 9), again discussing his readers using the grammatical third person instead of directly addressing them with second-person point of view.

> It is now time to look after Sophia; whom the reader, if he loves her half so well as I do, will rejoice to find escaped from the clutches of her passionate father, and from those of her dispassionate lover.

Second-person point of view allows you to directly address your audience, but as you see from these examples from Fielding's novel, you can also talk about your readers, without addressing them directly, in the grammatical third person.

The Novel's Audience: Second or Third Person?

Which is preferable when discussing your readers in your novel, second or third person? Of course, if you want to address your readers directly, use second-person point of view because it allows you to write as if you know them personally and are talking directly to them. If you want to talk *about* your readers rather than directly *to* them, use the grammatical third person when referring to them (which means you'll be writing in unlimited point of view or in a combination of unlimited and first person, as Fielding does in the previous examples). Talking about your readers in the grammatical third person creates a greater emotional distance between you and them than does using second-person point of view to directly address them.

SECOND-PERSON POINT OF VIEW IN CONTEMPORARY FICTION

There are quite a few short stories written using second-person point of view, including my own "Naked, With Glasses," as well as Margaret Atwood's "Rape Fantasies" and "Hair Jewelry," Anna Bianke's "Here You Are," Pam Houston's "How to Talk to a Hunter" and Brian Stanley Johnson's "Aren't You Rather Young to be Writing Your Memoirs?"

There are many contemporary novels that use second-person point of view, including Julian Barnes's *Flaubert's Parrot*, John

Barth's *Lost in the Funhouse*, Margaret Coombs's *Regards to the Czar*, Marguerite Duras's *The Malady of Death*, Günter Grass's *Cat and Mouse*, John Hawkes's *The Lime Twig* and *Travesty*, Thomas Keneally's *A Dutiful Daughter* and Kurt Vonnegut's *Breakfast of Champions*. As with other points of view, the best way to master second person is to become familiar with fiction that successfully uses it.

SECOND-PERSON POINT OF VIEW
IN COMMERCIAL FICTION

In commercial fiction, second-person point of view is often used to mean the generalized, nebulous audience, that is, all human beings or all humanity. In Susan Krinard's paranormal romance *Once a Wolf*, both the heroine and hero are werewolves, although the heroine tries to deny or suppress her werewolf heritage through much of the novel. At one point in chapter 10, when the hero is going to change into a wolf, the author switches to second-person point of view to indicate that she is talking about all werewolves, not just the hero (and certainly not about the readers).

> The fact was that being a werewolf meant you had the advantage over every other man. It meant you could smell a thousand times more keenly, move faster than human eyes could follow, hear a needle hit the floor from five rooms away. It meant you could always win, just by using powers you'd been born with but hadn't earned.

Second-person point of view is also used in commercial fiction when the narrator or another character is addressing another character within the novel although not in dialogue, as James Morrow did in his award-winning fantasy novel *Only Begotten Daughter*. Peter Straub employed the same technique in his horror novel *Mr. X*, when Mr. X, the antagonist and villain, addresses a group of implied characters. As Mr. X's feelings toward these implied characters change, so does his second-person address. In the early part of the novel (chapter 2), he calls them "O Great Old Ones" and refers to himself as their "Devoted Servant," but later (in chapter 115), bitter and disillusioned, he addresses them like this: "O

You Swarming ~~Majesties~~ Cruelties, Who Giveth with one hand and Taketh Away with the other."

FINAL WORDS ON SECOND-PERSON POINT OF VIEW

There's no limit to the number of times or the ways you can use second-person point of view in your novels. As McInerney's *Bright Lights, Big City* has proven, you can even write an entire novel in second person. Remember that using second-person point of view does not mean using "you" in dialogue when characters are speaking to each other. Second-person point of view means using "you" outside of dialogue. Although second-person point of view is rarer in commercial fiction than in literary fiction, it can still be used effectively in any genre.

In order to effectively use second-person point of view, be clear to whom the "you" is referring. Are you talking directly to your readers? Do you have a narrator talking to another character? Are you referring to all humanity in general? The "you" of second-person point of view can be any of these:

- the novel's reading audience
- the narrator's audience
- implied characters
- other actual characters in the novel
- humanity in general
- real persons outside the novel who are not the readers, for example, celebrities, politicians, etc.

Second-person point of view can add depth and complexity to your novel by emotionally involving the readers; they will feel you are talking directly to them. It can allow you to parody other novels that have used second person as well as to parody point of view in general (as many of the postmodernists do) by using it mockingly. It can help you create implied characters by addressing a "you" who is not your readers yet is not another actual character in the novel. It can allow you to make political commentary by addressing, for example, contemporary, living politicians who are not characters in your book. The possibilities are limitless.

As long as you are clear about the relationship of the "you" to the other characters in the novel and to your own audience, and as long as you have a legitimate reason for using second-person point of view, your readers will be able to understand what you're doing.

TIP Use second-person point of view if you want to talk directly to your readers and get them emotionally involved in the work. Combine second person with first person, using an interesting persona, if you want to express your own views of life, etc., in the novel and also address your readers.

EXERCISES FOR SECOND-PERSON POINT OF VIEW

1. Write a scene in unlimited point of view in which you interrupt the story to address your reading audience, using second-person point of view to talk directly to that audience. Make sure the scene has urgency and that there is a legitimate reason for addressing the audience, even if this reason is to parody the rest of the work in the scene (as postmodernists do). Maintain urgency when you return to unlimited point of view. Show your work to your readers to get their reactions and suggestions for improvement. Ask them how they felt when they were directly addressed in the scene. If their response was not the effect you'd hoped for, revise it and try again.

2. Write a scene in first-person point of view in which you interrupt the story to address your reading audience, using second-person point of view to talk directly to that audience. You may wish to adopt a persona (see chapter 3 on the difference between the persona, author and narrator). You may wish to create a self-reflexive or self-conscious narrator (see also chapter 3). Show it to your readers. If their response was not the effect you'd hoped for, revise it and try again.

3. Write a scene in inner limited point of view in which you interrupt the story to address your reading audience, using second-person point of view to talk directly to that audience. If their response was not the effect you'd hoped for, revise it and try again.

4. Write a scene in outer limited point of view (see chapter 6 for information on outer limited) in which you interrupt the story to

address your reading audience, using second-person point of view to talk directly to that audience. If their response was not the effect you'd hoped for, revise it and try again.

5. Write a scene in first-person point of view in which the narrator (who should be a character in this exercise and not you yourself) interrupts the story to address an audience other than your own audience, that is, not the audience of the novel in which the scene would appear. The "you" addressed by the narrator may be an actual character in the scene, an implied character, the author (that is, you) or anyone else you desire. Make sure the scene has urgency and that the narrator has a legitimate reason for interrupting it to address the audience. Maintain urgency when you return to your narrator's story in first-person point of view. Show it to your readers to get their reactions and suggestions for improvement. Ask them how they felt when your narrator used second-person point of view and whether your readers felt it was effective. If their response was not what you'd hoped for, revise it and try again.

SIX

OUTER LIMITED POINT OF VIEW

Whatever [point of view] you choose,
you should exploit the possibilities of the [point of view]
rather than feel constrained by its limitations.

JAMES N. FREY

How to Write a Damn Good Novel, II

Without a doubt the most challenging and difficult point of view for any novelist is outer limited. Also called the "fly-on-the-wall," the camera or the videotape point of view, outer limited requires the author to be completely objective—almost nonhumanly so—about the material she's presenting. The author writes in the grammatical third person and presents only the actions and objects she can observe externally. The point of view is limited to the outer behavior and actions of the characters. No unspoken thoughts, motivations, emotions or desires are presented. None. Not of any character. (And there's no voice-over in this camera point of view.)

The author is outside all characters at all times and never presents her characters' hidden or internal psychological lives. Everything about the characters must be presented externally, that is, if the characters don't express themselves aloud, the author must portray body language and behavior that reveal the characters' inner psychological and emotional states.

In order to maintain outer limited point of view, the author must be objective, nonjudgmental, emotionally uninvolved with the material, and completely neutral about the characters she's created and what happens to them. Yet every word an author chooses reveals her subjectivity and her emotional involvement with her created world.

For example, let's examine some instances of such subjectivity in word choice from my previous paragraphs. I originally wrote "inhumanly" for "nonhumanly," "emotionally distant" for "emotionally uninvolved" and "impersonal" for "neutral." All of those original choices—inhuman, emotionally distant and impersonal—carry negative connotations that imply the author's subjectivity, thus creating a lapse from outer limited point of view. Adjectives and adverbs can imply subjectivity, as can many of the dialogue tags authors use. That's one of the reasons it's so challenging to write in this point of view.

Though a daunting task, many authors have been artistically stimulated and excited about the very challenges presented by writing in outer limited point of view.

ADVANTAGES OF OUTER LIMITED POINT OF VIEW

Because the writer must remain outside his characters at all times and provides absolutely no interpretation of the events being presented, at least in the ideal version of outer limited point of view, the readers are forced to interpret the novel themselves. In other words, the readers are forced to become, at the very least, intellectually involved. Since most readers forced to interpret a novel's events and meanings reread the novel several times, they also become emotionally invested in the work. This could be considered an advantage.

There are thematic and symbolic advantages to using outer limited point of view as well. Since you do not present the characters' inner emotional or psychological lives, you can use this point of view as a metaphor for the individual isolation and spiritual alienation many people feel. Because the characters in the novel must communicate their emotions and thoughts for the readers to understand them as well as for other characters to understand them, unclear communication between characters can symbolically represent humankind's inability to express itself adequately or communicate effectively. Actually, the thematic and symbolic possibilities are endless; the examples I provide are merely a few.

Outer limited point of view is more common in literary fiction than in commercial fiction, though it is rare—in any genre—to find entire novels written in this point of view. Commercial detective and mystery fiction sometimes use outer limited for sections of the novel, as when presenting "taped" interrogations or trial transcripts.

Some advantages of using outer limited are for the writer himself rather than for his readers or the novel. It's artistically stimulating to write within self-imposed limitations. Because outer limited point of view has some of the most stringent limitations, writing in this point of view will stretch your skill as a writer and as an artist.

DISADVANTAGES OF OUTER LIMITED POINT OF VIEW

The most obvious disadvantage to writing in outer limited point of view, of course, is that some readers do not want to go through the work of interpreting a novel's events. They don't want to invest the emotional or intellectual energy involved in such a project. Such readers won't even finish the novel the first time, let alone reread it several times in order to interpret its events. Also, there's always the possibility that even if the readers like outer limited point of view and complete the novel, they won't feel any emotional attachment to the characters and what's happened to them because nothing of the characters' inner lives is ever revealed.

For the artist, the very thing that makes writing in outer limited point of view challenging and artistically stimulating is the same thing that makes it frustrating—its limitations. The author cannot present any judgment or subjectivity; therefore, it is extremely difficult to maintain this point of view for the length of an entire novel. Also, the author needs readers who are experienced in and literate enough about point of view to indicate lapses in point of view while the author is working on the novel and its revisions.

TIP Watch films with the sound turned off if you want some practice observing body language and nonverbals, which you'll need to master if you want to write successfully in outer limited point of view.

OUTER LIMITED POINT OF VIEW
IN LITERARY FICTION

One author who consistently attempted to write in outer limited point of view was Ernest Hemingway. His short story "Hills Like White Elephants" is an outstanding example of his use of outer limited point of view. (Hemingway only occasionally lapses into unlimited point of view in this story. More on that in chapter 10.)

> The hills across the Valley of the Ebro were long and white. On this side there was no shade and no trees and the station was between two lines of rails in the sun. Close against the side of the station there was the warm shadow of the building and a curtain, made of strings of bamboo beads, hung across the open door into the bar, to keep out flies. The American and the girl with him sat at a table in the shade, outside the building.

And here is another example from Hemingway's story "Big Two-Hearted River."

> The train went on up the track out of sight, around one of the hills of birch timber. Nick sat down on the bundle of canvas and bedding the baggage man had pitched out of the door of the baggage car. There was no town, nothing but the rails and burned over country. The thirteen saloons that had lined the one street . . . had not left a trace. The foundations of the . . . hotel stuck up above the ground. The stone was chipped and split by the fire. It was all that was left of the town. . . .

In both his short stories and his novels, Hemingway is a master at writing dialogue in outer limited point of view. Even if the remainder of the novel is written in unlimited or first person, Hemingway virtually always uses outer limited point of view when writing dialogue, so you can learn a great deal about this point of view by reading his dialogue.

The undisputed master of outer limited point of view, however,

---

TIP Only using the dialogue tags of "he said," "she said," is an easy way to write in outer limited point of view.

---

is French writer Alain Robbe-Grillet. In his novel *Jealousy*, Robbe-Grillet flawlessly maintains the impersonal, objective and non-judgmental outer limited point of view in 98 percent of the novel. The only time Robbe-Grillet leaves outer limited point of view in *Jealousy* is when he purposely slips into his ambiguously presented unlimited point of view (more about ambiguity in unlimited point of view in chapter 2). The novel is concerned with the actions of a wife—simply called A . . . in the novel—and her suspected lover as they are viewed by a jealous husband through a louvre shutter. Since the word for "jealousy" and for "louvre shutter" in French is the same—*jalousie*—even the book's title becomes ambiguous. (I have excerpted this at length since outer limited point of view is so challenging for writers of all skill levels.)

> A . . . is lying fully dressed on the bed. One of her legs rests on the satin spread; the other, bent at the knee, hangs half over the edge. The arm on this side is bent toward the head lying on the bolster. Stretched across the wide bed, the other arm lies out from the body at approximately a 45 degree angle. Her face is turned upward toward the ceiling. Her eyes are made still larger by the darkness. . . .
>
> She is sitting in the chair between the hallway door and the writing table. She is rereading a letter which shows the creases where it has been folded. Her long legs are crossed. Her right hand is holding the sheet in front of her face; her left hand is gripping the end of the armrest. . . .
>
> Between this first window and the second, there is just room enough for the large wardrobe. A . . ., who is standing beside it, is therefore visible only from the third window, the one that overlooks the west gable-end.

In outer limited point of view, since the author remains objective and apparently outside the story, it is the arrangement of the scenes and the details that reveals the novel's meaning and allows readers to interpret the characters and their behavior, as this excerpt from *Jealousy* demonstrates.

Though Robbe-Grillet's novel *In the Labyrinth* is mostly written in unlimited point of view (albeit ambiguous unlimited), there are several passages written in outer limited point of view, as in

> **TIP** Read Robbe-Grillet's novel *Jealousy* to really get an intuitive understanding and appreciation of outer limited point of view.

this passage describing the moment the wandering soldier of the novel arrives in a pseudo-barracks, which is also serving as a temporary infirmary for other soldiers. I have included this second example since this point of view is so challenging.

> The folded bedclothes form two dark rectangles against the lighter background of the mattress, two rectangles which overlap at one corner. The beds to the right and left are both occupied: two bodies lying on their backs, wrapped in their blankets; the heads are supported by bolsters of the same light shade as the mattresses; the man on the right has also put his hands under his neck, the folded elbows pointing diagonally on each side. The man is not sleeping: his eyes are wide open.

Many of the other so-called "new novelists" from France used outer limited point of view, if not exclusively, then periodically throughout their novels. Here is an example from Marguerite Duras's novel *Blue Eyes, Black Hair*. Though most of the novel is written in unlimited point of view, there are passages where Duras uses outer limited.

> There's another long pause before they speak again. She's standing in front of him. Her face is bare, without the black silk. He doesn't raise his eyes to her. He stays like that, without moving, for a long time. And then she leaves him, leaves the light, and goes along by the wall.

Outer limited is extremely difficult to do, but there are many literary authors who do it extremely effectively. As long as you stay completely out of all the characters' heads—presenting only their outer lives, their external, observable behavior—and provide no subjective interpretation of the novel's action, you will be writing in outer limited point of view.

OUTER LIMITED POINT OF VIEW
IN COMMERCIAL FICTION

Although lengthy or sustained examples of outer limited point of view most often appear in literary fiction, there are occasionally shorter passages or examples of it in commercial fiction. Most often the passages written in outer limited point of view appear in detective, mystery or suspense novels, most notably in sections imitating the transcripts of trial proceedings or police interrogations. Here's an example from chapter 15 of Ed McBain's 87th Precinct police procedural *Kiss*:

> *Q:* How did you let yourself in?
>
> *A:* I had a key.
>
> *Q:* A key to the inner lobby door?
>
> *A:* Yes. And also the keys to the apartment. There are two locks on the apartment door.
>
> *Q:* Where'd you get all these keys?
>
> *A:* Emma gave them to me. I spent a weekend with her when Bowles was out of town. That's when she gave me the keys.
>
> *Q:* So you waited for the doorman to take his dinner break . . .
>
> *A:* His *coffee* break. Watched him walking up the street . . .
>
> *Q:* And then you let yourself in the building . . .
>
> *A:* Yes.

The author doesn't tell us who's asking or answering the questions, even when the suspect's lawyer interrupts the police during the interrogation. It's clear from the content of the questions and answers who is speaking. No body language is presented, no adjectives or adverbs, nothing that would indicate any interpretation or subjective depiction of the scene. It's pure outer limited point of view.

TIP Like writing dialogue-only passages, writing scenes in the form of a transcript, which is in outer limited point of view, is an excellent way to develop your dialogue skills.

FINAL WORDS ON OUTER LIMITED POINT OF VIEW

In outer limited point of view, the author stays completely outside his characters, limiting his presentation to their outer lives. He writes in the grammatical third person and never reveals the unspoken thoughts, emotions or motivations of any character. The author must use descriptions of behavior or dialogue to reveal personalities of his characters. Because of these stringent limitations, outer limited is the most challenging and difficult point of view to maintain for any length of time. These limitations, however, can force the readers to become more emotionally involved in the work itself and can be artistically stimulating for the author.

TIP Even if you don't want to write your entire novel (or entire chapters, sections, etc.) in outer limited point of view, doing exercises involving your novel's characters and writing those exercises in outer limited point of view can give you insight into their behavior, including body language and nonverbals. You can then add the description of their behavior to the rest of the scene, no matter what point of view the novel is ultimately written in.

EXERCISES FOR OUTER LIMITED POINT OF VIEW

1. Rent a video you have never seen and with whose story you are not familiar. Watch the video with the sound turned off. Watch at least one scene several times. Without turning on the sound, try to write exactly what you see in the scene, using outer limited point of view. Watch the characters' actions and behaviors closely. Pay special attention to their body language and nonverbals so that you can describe it in great detail. Write this scene without judgment, that is, as an objective observer, a "fly on the wall" or a video camera. Present all characters in the scene equally sympathetically so that the reader understands the actions, behavior and motivations of all the characters equally, even if the reader doesn't approve of them. Show the scene to your readers and ask them specifically to see if they can determine your emotional involvement or feelings about the characters in the scene. If any emo-

tional subjectivity is revealed, ask them which words betray it. Eliminate or change those words.

2. Now watch the scene from exercise 1 with the sound on so you can hear the dialogue (if any). Rewrite the scene, with dialogue, but still in outer limited point of view. Do not use any adjectives, adverbs or special verbs for the dialogue tags: Use only "he said" or "she said." Let the emotion be in the dialogue itself, not in the tags. You may have to modify your description of their body language and their nonverbals to more accurately reflect their emotions after you have added the dialogue. Show the scene to your readers and ask them which words betray emotional subjectivity. Eliminate or change those words.

3. In a public place, observe the interaction of at least two people from a distance. Do not get close enough either to hear what they're saying or to determine the tone of their voices. Write down everything they're doing, paying special attention to body language so that you can describe it in great detail. Write this scene in outer limited point of view. Show the scene to your readers and ask them which words betray emotional subjectivity. Eliminate or change those words.

4. On a separate page, analyze what you think the body language of the people you observed in exercise 3 means. What is their relationship to each other? How well do they know each other? Are they intimate—sexually, emotionally, physically—with each other? What emotion is each person in the interaction feeling? Are these people tense, angry, happy, bored, sleepy, annoyed, irritable, amused, tolerant, etc.? How do you know this, that is, what body gestures and nonverbal signals indicate these emotions to you? Be aware of the types of body language and nonverbal signals by which people demonstrate their inner, emotional states so that you can use this information in your writing.

5. Give the observation you have written for exercise 3 to your readers (but do not give them your analysis). Ask the readers to analyze the body language in the scene you have written and to determine the relationships, moods, feelings, etc., of the characters you have described. If the readers do not come up with the same analysis that you did, ask them why. What body language that you described caused different interpretations? Rewrite the

scene until your readers interpret the body language you have described in the same way that you did.

6. Pick any emotion—love, hate, fear, courage, annoyance, surprise, disbelief, etc.—and write a scene in outer limited point of view showing that emotion without revealing to your readers what the emotion is. For this exercise do not use dialogue or have your character talking aloud to himself. Do not reveal any of the character's thoughts or unspoken feelings. Show only the character's behavior. Show actions that will reveal his emotional state to your readers. Do not title the scene or in any other way indicate what emotion you are describing. Show the scene to your readers and ask them to interpret the character's emotions. If your readers do not guess the emotion correctly, revise the scene accordingly.

7. Do exercise 6 again in outer limited point of view, only this time include dialogue if there is more than one character or, if the character is alone in the scene, have the character speak aloud to himself. (Remember that the character must be speaking aloud for the readers to know any of his thoughts or feelings since outer limited point of view does not show characters' minds.) If your readers do not guess the emotion correctly, revise the scene accordingly.

8. Do exercise 6 or 7 again in outer limited point of view, only this time do it entirely in dialogue. Use only "he said" or "she said" for dialogue tags. (In other words, do not use tags such as "he yelled," "she shrieked" or "he whined.") If your readers do not guess the emotion correctly, revise the scene accordingly.

SEVEN

COMBO POINT OF VIEW

Choices about point of view will undoubtedly be the most important decisions about technique that [an author] has to make.

RUST HILLS

Writing in General and the Short Story in Particular

Combo point of view, also called limited omniscient or floating, variable, flexible and revolving third-person point of view, combines sections of the novel written in unlimited point of view with sections written in inner limited. Because combo point of view appears most frequently in mystery, detective or suspense novels and because it has acquired the status of convention in terms of which characters are portrayed in unlimited point of view and which ones are in inner limited, it is often considered a separate and unique point of view.

In commercial fiction, unlimited point of view is used for the amateur sleuths, detectives, police, FBI agents or other crime-fighters and protagonists in these novels. In the passages or chapters of the novel written in unlimited point of view, the author moves freely among all characters, providing his readers with all thoughts, unspoken motivations, emotions and desires of all the characters. There are no limitations to the information the author can present in these sections of the novel. In combo point of view, however, unlimited is reserved for use when presenting the crime-fighters.

Inner limited point of view is used for the victims (usually during the commission of the crime), the killers or criminals in these novels. In the passages or chapters written in inner limited point of view, the author chooses one character—either the victim or the criminal—and reveals all the thoughts, feelings and motivations of that character. The author writes about that character in the grammatical third person, using he, she, it or they to refer to the chosen character and revealing only the external, observable behavior of the other characters in those same scenes.

In the inner limited sections of the novel, the author stays out of the heads of all the characters except the one he has chosen. That means that if the author chooses to be in the victim's head during the depiction of a murder, the author does not portray the murderer's thoughts, feelings or motivations in that specific scene. (The author may, however, choose to do so in another section of the novel, which would also be written in inner limited point of view.) Conversely, if the author chooses to be inside the killer's head in any particular scene, the author would not portray the victim's thoughts, feelings or motivations in that scene, although he may do so in another section of the novel also written in inner limited point of view.

This switching of point of view between unlimited to portray the crime-fighters and inner limited to depict the criminals or their victims adds tension to the novel in several ways. First of all, unlimited point of view reassures readers emotionally by subtly reminding them that the author is in charge of whatever happens in the novel. Changing to inner limited point of view during the more violent episodes—whether the violence is physical or psychological—takes away the readers' safety net, so to speak, increasing their emotional vulnerability and heightening the dramatic tension. Also, inner limited point of view allows the readers to have a glimpse into the minds of either the criminals or their victims, which also increases the dramatic tension. Returning to unlimited point of view for the crime-fighters prevents the readers' emotional vulnerability from becoming unbearable and also reassures them that things in the novel will turn out according to the genre expectations. (Of course, readers may not be able to articulate this emotional vulnerability or safety since it operates at a deeper, more subconscious level, but the author needs to be aware of this potential.)

ADVANTAGES OF COMBO POINT OF VIEW

The greatest advantage of combo point of view is its flexibility. The author moves at will into and out of the heads of his protago-

nists, while limiting the readers' access to psychological motivations during the depiction of the crime scenes. Writing in inner
limited point of view is especially popular in commercial fiction
for depicting the criminal's psychological state since it prevents
the readers from identifying too closely with the criminal, as
would happen if the author used first-person point of view. In commercial fiction written in combo point of view, the readers' sympathy is always clearly directed toward the crime-fighters rather than
toward the criminals. In contemporary literary fiction, for example, authors most often use first-person point of view when depicting the criminal mind for exactly the reason it is not used in commercial fiction: It creates greater sympathy for the criminal.

Another advantage to using inner limited point of view for the
criminal is that by writing about the criminal in the grammatical
third person and in this limited point of view, you can add suspense to the novel by not revealing the criminal's identity until
later in the book.

In the case of commercial crime novels, the choice of inner limited point of view for the criminals clearly serves to keep the readers from becoming too emotionally involved or from feeling connected to the criminals; using inner limited for the victims allows
the readers to reconstruct the crime scene just as professional
crime-fighters do.

THE DISADVANTAGE OF COMBO POINT OF VIEW

The disadvantage of combo point of view, especially the inner limited sections, would be the emotional distance it creates between
the readers and the characters. Although this may be preferable
when portraying the criminal, it may be a disadvantage when portraying the victim.

COMBO POINT OF VIEW IN LITERARY FICTION

Combo point of view, that is, novels restricted to unlimited point
of view when portraying crime-fighting protagonists and inner limited point of view when portraying criminals or their victims, most
often occurs in commercial fiction. When authors of literary fiction use unlimited and inner limited points of view, they do not
restrict the use of a particular point of view to a certain type of

character, as does commercial crime fiction. Also, literary authors often combine these points of view with first and second person, so these authors and their works will be discussed in chapter 9 on multiple points of view.

COMBO POINT OF VIEW IN COMMERCIAL FICTION

Combo point of view has become extremely popular in commercial crime or suspense fiction where the victims or criminals are presented in inner limited point of view. Here is an example of the killer's perspective, from chapter 1 of Tami Hoag's *Ashes to Ashes*:

> He lifts the body from the back of the Blazer like a roll of old carpet to be discarded. . . . He has spent many hours, days, months, years studying his compulsion [to kill] and its point of origin. He knows what he is, and he embraces that truth. He has never known guilt or remorse.

Hoag also uses inner limited point of view for the victims in this novel (also from chapter 1).

> She ran, her lungs burning, her legs burning, her eyes burning, her throat burning. In one abstract corner of her mind, she was the corpse. . . . The cop was beside her in an instant, holstering his weapon and dropping to his knees to help. Must be a rookie, she thought dimly. She knew fourteen-year-old kids with better street instincts. She could have got his weapon. If she'd had a knife, she could have raised herself up and stabbed him.

TIP Using inner limited point of view for victims in a crime novel allows you and your readers to think like the police and other crime investigators do. By putting yourself in the victim's place and writing from his perspective—but using the grammatical third person rather than switching to first-person point of view—you will gain more insight into the psyches of your crime-fighters as well.

For the crime-fighters in *Ashes to Ashes*—the police, the attorneys and the protagonist (a former FBI agent turned victim-witness advocate)—Hoag uses unlimited point of view, as this excerpt from chapter 2 illustrates:

> The only thing [protagonist Kate Conlan] had wished for all the way home from . . . Las Vegas was a return to the nice, normal, relatively sane life she had made for herself. . . .
>
> Lunch hours and evenings found [the county attorney] moving among the Minneapolis power elite, currying connections and favor. It was common knowledge he had his eye on a seat in the US Senate.

Hoag moves freely inside and outside her characters' heads when she portrays the crime-fighters, thus using unlimited point of view.

Other suspense/mystery writers also use combo point of view. Ed McBain uses it in his police procedurals. In his novel *Kiss*, he uses inner limited for the victim's perspective and unlimited point of view for the police.

There are also many suspense and mystery novels that use inner limited point of view for the killers or their victims and then first-person point of view for the crime-fighters. These novels are discussed in chapter 9 on multiple points of view.

TIP Using combo point of view gets you all the advantages of unlimited point of view, where you write without any limitations or restrictions, and yet allows you to penetrate the mind of criminals or killers without seeming to morally approve of their behavior. It also prevents your readers from becoming too emotionally involved with the criminals, since the use of inner limited point of view creates emotional distance between the readers and the character.

FINAL WORDS ON COMBO POINT OF VIEW

Combo point of view has become extremely popular in commercial fiction, especially in crime fiction. To use combo point of view, present the protagonists—the crime-fighters—in your crime novel in unlimited point of view and present the victims or the criminals in inner limited point of view. There are no restrictions or limitations to the information you can present in the sections of the novel written in unlimited point of view. To write the passages in inner limited point of view well, you must master all the limitations of first-person point of view, but write about your characters in the grammatical third person.

EXERCISES FOR COMBO POINT OF VIEW

1. Write a scene in inner limited point of view from a crime victim's perspective. You may write the scene so that it takes place before, during or after the commission of the crime. Present the victim's thoughts, feelings and unspoken motivations, but talk about the victim using the grammatical third person: he, she, it, they. For any other characters in the scene, you must remain outside their heads, that is, you may only present directly observable behavior, dialogue or other spoken words. Show the scene to your readers for their feedback and suggestions for improvement.

2. Write the scene from exercise 1 over again in inner limited point of view, this time from the criminal's perspective. Present the criminal's thoughts, feelings and unspoken motivations, but only the external behavior and dialogue of the other characters. Show the scene to your readers for their feedback and suggestions for improvement.

3. Now write about the scene from exercises 1 and 2, this time from the crime-fighters' perspective, using unlimited point of view. You may move freely in and out of all the crime-fighters' heads in this exercise (but not into the criminal's head, if he is in this scene). Show the scene to your readers for their feedback and suggestions for improvement.

4. Combine all of the three scenes from exercises 1, 2 and 3 above into one coherent segment of a novel. You will have to decide which scene to present first, where the criminal's perspective should go in relation to the victim's, etc. Try several arrangements of the scenes until you have the most effective arrangement possible. Show the segment to your readers for their feedback and suggestions for improvement.

EIGHT

CREATING CHALLENGING PERSPECTIVES AND EXPERIMENTING WITH POINT OF VIEW

The "rules" [about point of view] can be broken, of course, if the violation isn't noticeable, or if enough is achieved by doing so; but to break the rules of point of view unwittingly, with nothing accomplished by it, is to harm the story foolishly.

RUST HILLS

Writing in General and the Short Story in Particular

Challenging perspectives are not so much new or unique points of view as they are interesting or unusual variations on existing points of view. This chapter does not encompass all the possibilities of challenging perspectives; instead, it examines a few of the more famous or popular ones.

Most of the challenging perspectives can be found in literary fiction although a surprising amount of the experimentation eventually makes its way into commercial fiction. Of course, as an author, you need to be aware of the fact that if the perspective is too challenging or experimental, it will prevent your readers from understanding the novel (or even prevent the readers from finishing the novel), and then you may have a difficult time getting the novel published. If you do manage to get it published despite its difficult or experimental nature, you may have a problem keeping it in print since very few people may buy it. However, as many literary and commercial authors have shown, you can use challenging perspectives and experiment with point of view quite successfully as long as you tell a good story and create memorable characters at the same time.

All challenging perspectives involve a great deal of research, introspection on the author's part and an ability to access the artistic subconscious. Experimenting with point of view involves the same kind of research and introspection; therefore, you might want to read chapter 10, "Voice and Artistic Intuition," and do some of the intuition-enhancing exercises before you attempt a more challenging perspective or experiment with point of view.

ADVANTAGES OF CHALLENGING PERSPECTIVES

The greatest advantage to a challenging perspective or experimenting with point of view is that such work advances art formally. In other words, experiments in perspective or point of view advance the "form" of the literature. This can be done by stretching the current boundaries of the genre, by experimenting with language itself or by changing the expectations of a particular point of view. Thus, when an author successfully writes a contemporary romance in first person rather than in the traditionally used unlimited point of view, the author is making a formal advance in that genre. Similarly, when authors began making their narrators unreliable as storytellers, these authors were making a formal advance in first-person point of view.

When you make formal advances in literature, either in the genre format or in point of view, other authors then want to imitate your work; reviewers and critics pay special attention to your novel. It is also artistically stimulating and can help you grow as an artist. Furthermore, some readers, especially those who read literary fiction, want to be intellectually challenged and are excited about interesting variations or innovations in art.

THE DISADVANTAGE OF CHALLENGING PERSPECTIVES

The disadvantage to using challenging perspectives or experimenting with point of view is that it may alienate—or even eliminate—the readers.

PSYCHOLOGICALLY OR EMOTIONALLY IMPAIRED PERSPECTIVES

Ever since first becoming interested in creating characters who were realistic, authors have been writing about psychologically or emotionally impaired characters. Authors often use first-person

TIP Read literary fiction to discover the most famous representations of challenging perspectives. Some of the novels with the most challenging perspectives, such as Dostoevsky's *Notes from the Underground* or Faulkner's *The Sound and the Fury*, are now considered "modern" rather than "avant-garde," though these novels were considered quite shocking when they were first published.

point of view for novels with these characters so there will be an intense emotional identification between the readers and the character. Psychological or emotional impairment, however, makes the narrator unreliable. The more psychologically or emotionally impaired the narrator is, the more unreliable she is.

Notes from the Underground

Dostoevsky's *Notes from the Underground*, narrated by the unnamed Underground Man, presents readers with a narrator who constantly changes his story and who insists, almost pathologically, that he's a liar (from part 1, chapter 1).

> I am a sick man . . . I am a spiteful man. I am an unattractive man. I believe my liver is diseased. However, I know nothing at all about my disease, and do not know for certain what ails me.

And later in that same chapter, he tells us,

> I was lying when I said just now that I was a spiteful official. I was lying from spite. I was simply amusing myself with the petitioners and with the officer, and in reality I never could become spiteful.

Then in part 1, chapter 9, the Underground Man changes his story once again.

> Gentlemen, I'm joking, and I know myself that my jokes are not brilliant, but you know one can't take everything as a joke. . . . Lies, lies, lies! Of course I have myself made up all the things you say. That, too, is from underground.

Not only is the Underground Man unreliable because he's lying, but his first-person narrative is interspersed with second-person point of view when he addresses the gentlemen of his audience and then insists that of course he's making up his audience and everything his audience says. Dostoevsky effectively uses a challenging perspective and experimented with point of view, much as postmodern novelists do.

Final Words on Notes from the Underground

It's relatively easy to create an unreliable narrator who's lying. What's difficult is creating a lying narrator who's memorable and likable at the same time that he tells us he's lying. Dostoevsky does just that.

TIP The more you know about human psychology, the easier it will be to create challenging perspectives.

The Sound and the Fury

William Faulkner's masterpiece *The Sound and the Fury* presents us with two psychologically challenged narrators: Benjy, a thirty-something man retarded to the age of three; and his brother Quentin, who is suicidal and kills himself at the end of his section of the novel. As you can imagine, both of these narrators are extremely unreliable due to their psychological impairments. Quentin is extremely depressed, pessimistic and obsessed with his incestuous love for his sister Caddy. Since Quentin is on his way to commit suicide, his interior monologue during his trip to the river where he will drown himself is interspersed with his extremely unreliable memories of family events and relationships (from the section titled "June Second, 1910").

> And so as soon as I knew I couldn't see [the clock], I began to wonder what time it was. . . . Excrement Father said like sweating. And I saying All right. Wonder. Go on and wonder. . . . I said I have committed incest, Father I said.

Quentin, though he is not retarded, is as unreliable as his brother Benjy.

Benjy, the "idiot" alluded to in the title, which is taken from Shakespeare, views the world and relates to the people in his world as a three-year-old child would: through his senses and his rather labile emotions. Despite Benjy's sometimes using an extremely sophisticated vocabulary in his interior monologue, which indicates Faulkner's few lapses in point of view (more on that in chapter 10), Benjy is actually the most reliable narrator in the novel.

Encountering this scene for the first time, many readers do not understand what Benjy is telling them (from "April Seventh, 1928").

> I got undressed and I looked at myself, and I began to cry. Hush, Luster said. Looking at them ain't going to do no good. They're gone. You keep on like this, and we ain't going have you no more birthday.

Later, when Quentin refers to Benjy as a "eunuch" and Jason calls him "the Great American Gelding," we understand what Benjy was telling us—he was castrated. Faulkner has brilliantly used first-person point of view, limiting the event to Benjy's perception and understanding of the traumatic event. Because Benjy tells us his emotions as well as the physical aspects of the castration, he becomes the most reliable narrator of the three brothers. Throughout his first-person narrative, he tells the readers more of the truth than anyone else because he does not judge what he sees the other characters doing but simply reports it.

The third Compson brother, Jason, is not psychologically impaired, but he is still quite unreliable. The opening of Jason's part of the novel tells the readers everything they need to know about his personality (from "April Sixth, 1928").

> Once a bitch always a bitch, what I say. I says you're lucky if her playing out of school is all that worries you. I says she ought to be down there in that kitchen right now, instead of up there in her room, gobbing paint on her face and waiting for six niggers that can't even stand up out of a chair unless they've got a pan full of bread and meat to balance them, to fix breakfast for her.

Bitter, misogynistic, misanthropic, racist. That's Jason. He hates everyone but himself, and he sees himself as the maligned and misunderstood victim of the rest of his family's machinations and moral mistakes. Because this section is written in first-person point of view, however, and because readers are limited to seeing the world the way Jason himself sees it, readers develop a type of empathy for Jason. It's a tribute to Faulkner's artistry that Jason, undeniably one of the most hateful characters in literature, is also one of the funniest and most sympathetic in the novel. Although most readers wouldn't want to have Jason in their own family, they understand why he feels the way he does and, at times, feel sorry for him. This is accomplished through the intimacy of first-person point of view.

Final Words on *The Sound and the Fury*

This is absolutely the masterpiece if you want to do challenging perspectives or multiple perspectives on the same events. Despite the occasional lapses in point of view, Faulkner accurately presents psychologically and emotionally impaired narrators, brilliantly using first-person point of view throughout the first three sections of the novel, then switching to unlimited point of view for the final section.

TIP Creating perspectives that are noticeably different from each other can be just as challenging as creating narrators who are psychologically impaired. For an analysis of the different ways men and women communicate and think, read Deborah Tannen's *You Just Don't Understand*. Then incorporate some of her findings into your novel when portraying male and female perspectives.

The Waterfall

Margaret Drabble's novel *The Waterfall* uses inner limited point of view through at least half of the novel as we learn of the protagonist's adulterous affair with her cousin's husband, James. Before the affair has started, Jane tells us of her husband's "desertion."

> Some weeks later, he left. She was not surprised. She'd been expecting it. She was quite pleased to see him go. Everything seemed a little colder without him.

Partway through the novel, the author switches to first-person point of view as Jane now becomes the narrator.

> It's obvious that I haven't told the truth, about myself and James. . . . And yet I haven't lied. I've merely omitted: merely, professionally, edited. This is dishonest, but not as dishonest as deliberate falsehood.

She claims to be unreliable, telling us that she's left out many important parts of the story, but then she proceeds to tell us all of those details she claims to have previously omitted. The novel continues in this fashion, with Jane always telling the readers, in the first-person sections, everything she's previously "omitted" in the inner limited sections. She even mocks herself and the writing process at one point, saying,

> I'm getting tired of all this Freudian [analysis of my family and our relationship]; I want to get back to that schizoid third-person dialogue.

Final Words on *The Waterfall*

Despite the fact that in the first-person passages the narrator claims to be unreliable, saying she omitted some of the facts in the inner limited passages, by providing us with the omissions in the first-person sections, she ultimately becomes a reliable narrator. It's an extremely challenging perspective—a narrator who claims to be lying and claims to be unreliable but who, ultimately, is extremely reliable. And the novel also combines two different points of view. Drabble carries it all off splendidly.

Other Psychologically/Emotionally Impaired Perspectives

There are many examples of psychologically or emotionally impaired perspectives, in literary and commercial fiction, in first-person and in inner limited points of view. Spider of Patrick McGrath's *Spider* has schizophrenia and has murdered his mother. Francie of Patrick McCabe's *The Butcher Boy* is psychologically unsound and murders a neighbor because of imagined slights. Eleanor of my novel *Only With the Heart* has Alzheimer's, and her narrative takes place after the disease is quite advanced.

OTHER CHALLENGING PERSPECTIVES

Narrators do not have to be mentally ill or psychologically unsound to be unreliable. Any character who is in denial about some aspect of her life or her own behavior presents an artistically challenging perspective. Paula Spencer of Roddy Doyle's *The Woman Who Walked Into Doors* is being abused by her husband and is suffering from the denial typical of abused wives. Marcus Brennan, the lawyer-narrator of Frederick Busch's *Closing Arguments*, has so many secrets that he invents stories to hide them. Patrick McGrath's Edward Haggard (*Dr. Haggard's Disease*) cannot come to terms with his repressed homosexuality. Jay McInerney's "Coach" (*Bright Lights, Big City*), as his best friend calls him, is addicted to cocaine. Stephen King's uneducated Dolores (*Dolores Claiborne*) is accused of murdering her husband. Criminal narrators are often unreliable and not always because they're lying. There are as many reasons for narrators to be unreliable as there are unreliable narrators. Each one of these reasons creates an artistic challenge for the author.

TIP Read Carol Tavris's *Anger: The Misunderstood Emotion* for excellent examples of behavior and nonverbals that you can incorporate into your novel when creating characters with challenging perspectives.

Child Narrators

Children are always unreliable narrators even if they're not mentally retarded like Benjy in Faulkner's novel. From Mark Twain's Huck Finn (*The Adventures of Huckleberry Finn*) and Kaye Gibbons's Ellen (*Ellen Foster*) to Roddy Doyle's Paddy (*Paddy Clarke Ha Ha Ha*) and Anthony Burgess's Alex (*A Clockwork Orange*), child narrators, no matter what their age, are unreliable, though not necessarily intentionally so. Children are unreliable narrators simply because of their lack of experience or their limited knowledge of human behavior. Even when children believe they are telling the absolute and complete truth, they're only telling the truth as they know it; because of their limited experience or age, this makes them unreliable.

To Create Challenging Perspectives

To create challenging perspectives, whether in first-person or inner limited points of view, you need to research, observe, and then research and observe some more. After you are completely intellectually familiar with the behavior and thought processes of your challenging perspective, through nonfiction books, scholarly articles and interviews with authorities in the field, you need to become emotionally familiar with it. And that means observing. If you have to volunteer to work in a mental institution to become familiar with such characters, do so. You could volunteer or spend time in a prison, a rehab center, a halfway house, a children's daycare, an adult daycare, an assisted living unit. Many of the officials who work with mentally or emotionally challenged populations are excited about having novels written from those characters' perspectives, and are therefore extremely helpful and will assist you in doing your research.

After you have completed your observations, you need to do some of the meditation and intuition-enhancing exercises listed in chapter 10. Then, start writing.

LAYERED NARRATIVES

Layered narratives have more than one story contained within another. Mary Shelley's *Frankenstein* is an example of a layered first-person narrative. The first narrator, Captain Walton, discovers the creature when sailing to the North Pole. The creature, who is hunting Dr. Frankenstein, tells Captain Walton about being created. Captain Walton is writing letters to another character, telling her about the creature's story. Because one character is interpreting another character's story, the chances of unreliability greatly increase in layered narratives.

Another example of a layered narrative is Emily Brontë's *Wuthering Heights*, which is also layered first-person narratives. Mr. Lockwood rents a house from Mr. Heathcliff. When Mr. Lockwood becomes ill and is confined to bed, his housekeeper, Nelly Dean, tells him the love story of Heathcliff (when he was much younger) and Catherine. Because Mr. Lockwood is telling us the story that Nelly Dean has told him, the stories about Heathcliff and Catherine are extremely unreliable. In fact, the readers learn more about Nelly Dean's and Lockwood's personalities and worldview than they do about Cathy's and Heathcliff's love story. Most readers, upon first reading *Wuthering Heights*, do not notice the improbability of Nelly Dean's being with Catherine and Heathcliff (or in very close proximity to them) during some of their most intimate and private moments.

In addition to Brontë's *Wuthering Heights* and Shelley's *Frankenstein*, there are other layered narratives in literary fiction, including William Faulkner's *Absalom! Absalom!* and Günter Grass's *Dog Years*. In commercial fiction, Stephen King's *Misery* offers a layered narrative, both written in unlimited point of view. The protagonist Paul and his experiences with his captor, Annie, form one of the narratives, while Paul's story of Misery, the protagonist of one of his novels, forms the layered narrative.

To Create Layered Narratives

Layering first-person narratives can lead to extremely interesting and exciting character development. Make sure, however, that you develop each narrator as fully as possible into a realistic human being.

Also, be aware of the fact that it will be extremely challenging to present different voices for each of the narrators, especially when their stories are within other narrators' stories. For example, the various stories in *Frankenstein* have the same voice throughout, despite the fact that one is told by an educated sea captain and one by Frankenstein's creature.

LAYERED PERSPECTIVES

In addition to having layered narratives, you can present layered perspectives. One of the ways to do this is to present a character looking back on himself at an earlier point in his life, such as an adult character telling of himself and his behavior as a child. The challenge with this perspective is to make sure that you include that character's adult view of himself and his child's view at the same time.

Several authors have done this, including James Joyce in his short story "Araby," where the narrator looks back on himself as a young boy, when he suffered from an unrequited crush on Mangan's sister. Throughout the story, Joyce's narrator looks kindly and lovingly back on his younger self, presenting us with a layered perspective.

> I imagined that I bore my chalice [containing her "sacred" image] safely through a throng of foes. Her name sprang to my lips . . . in strange prayers . . . which I myself did not understand. My eyes were often full of tears (I could not tell why). . . . I pressed the palms of my hands together until they trembled, murmuring: *O love! O love!* many times.

It is the adult narrator who likens himself as a young boy to a priest, carrying the image of his loved one around in the metaphorical chalice. Thus we have the adult perspective of his own behavior when he was a boy: His love for this girl was so devout it became spiritual. And although the adult narrator knows why his eyes were full of tears when he was a young boy, he does not tell us, thus providing us with the perspective of himself as a young boy at the same time. Though written entirely in first-person point of view, it is this combination of both the adult and the child perspectives that makes this story so exciting and challenging.

This type of challenging perspective can be carried out for an entire novel. Charles Dickens does exactly this in *Great Expectations*. The adult Pip often reflects compassionately on his younger, more naïve self (from chapter 1).

> Since that time, which is far enough away now, I have often thought that few people know what secrecy there is in the young, under terror. No matter how unreasonable the terror, so that it be terror. I was in mortal terror of the [escaped convict] who wanted my heart and liver. . . ; I had no hope of deliverance through my all-powerful sister, who repulsed me at every turn. . . .

Other works presenting this layered perspective are William Faulkner's *The Reivers*, Marguerite Duras's *The Lover*, Günter Grass's *Cat and Mouse* and *The Tin Drum* and Chris Bohjalian's *Midwives*. Of course, any narrator looking back on herself at an earlier time in her life will have this same effect, so your narrator does not have to be remembering herself as a child. As long as you present both the current and the former views of the self, then you will be layering the perspective.

To Create Characters Looking Back
on Their Earlier Selves

To create believable characters or narrators who are looking back on their earlier selves, you must clearly understand how these characters/narrators view their younger or changed selves. Are they nostalgic? Sentimental? Bitter? Judgmental? Angry? Tolerant? Amazed? You may have to do some meditation or intuition exercises in order to clearly and accurately understand how your character/narrator views her previous self. No matter what point of view you decide to write in, you then have to ensure that the readers will be aware of this dual or multiple perspective. Read the authors who have mastered layered perspectives and notice how they portray the character's/narrator's changing attitudes toward herself.

INVENTING LANGUAGE

Much of postmodernist fiction struggles or plays with language, reflects upon the act of writing itself, and muses on the role of author and audience with respect to a novel. Sometimes authors have even invented a new language for their novels. Science fiction and fantasy writers often do this, especially when they're creating the worlds that existed before contemporary history, alternate history worlds or civilizations on other planets. Frank Herbert's *Dune* and Jean M. Auel's *The Clan of the Cave Bear* are examples of this.

Literary fiction, too, has its authors who invent language for their novels. The opening of James Joyce's *Finnegan's Wake* is as unusual and difficult to understand today as it was in 1939, when it was first published: "riverrun, past Eve's and Adam's, from swerve of shore to bend of bay, brings us by a commodious vicus of recirculation back to Howth Castle and Environs."

When Anthony Burgess invented a new language for his novel *A Clockwork Orange,* he was much more effective. Some copies of the novel are printed with the glossary in the back, but most readers have no difficulty figuring out what Burgess means, even without a glossary. The novel is in first-person point of view, but it is

Burgess's new language that makes his exploration of society and human behavior a challenging perspective. Not only does the new language cushion the extreme violence in the novel, but it makes the readers see the novel's world in a new way simply because it presents new words for familiar concepts. Here's the opening:

> There was me, that is Alex, and my three droogs, that is Pete, Georgie, and Dim, Dim being really dim, and we sat in the Korova Milkbar making up our rassoodocks what to do with the evening, a flip dark chill winter bastard though dry. The Korova Milkbar was a milk-plus mesto, and you may, O my brothers, have forgotten what these mestos were like, things changing so skorry these days and everybody very quick to forget, newspapers not being read much neither.

Readers usually figure out what individual words mean, but even if they can't, they understand that Alex and his buddies, who form a gang, are in a bar that serves milk with drugs because, as we learn later, it has no license for alcohol. Readers can also determine that Alex is aware of himself as a storyteller and has a specific audience, which he addresses—in second-person point of view—as "O my brothers." The familiarity of first-person point of view allows the readers immediate intimacy with the narrator, Alex.

A Clockwork Orange is a very exciting novel, and Burgess's invented language is what makes it so exciting because it allows the readers to re-examine, through the novel's new language, their own moral judgments on violence. The intimacy of the first-person point of view may, in fact, be the very thing that makes this invented language accessible to readers. If the novel had been written in unlimited point of view, for example, the readers would have felt more emotionally distant from the protagonist, Alex, and may have seen the invented language as a game on the part of the author. In first-person point of view, however, readers assume that much of the language is Alex's teenage slang and may be more tolerant of his linguistic games. If your only experience with this work is the Stanley Kubrick film, I urge you to read the novel to experience it in all its linguistic and moral complexity. If you want to invent a new language for your novel, reading *A Clockwork Orange* is a good place to start.

EXPERIMENTING WITH POINT OF VIEW

To experiment with point of view, you need to master point of view first, then read work by the postmodernists and others who've experimented with it. Then, simply experiment. Not everything you try will necessarily work or be completely effective. That's the nature of experiments. Many postmodern and experimental novelists claim that you must throw away things such as plot, character development, etc., in order to do something really dramatic and exciting with point of view. They may be right, but not having a plot also can alienate the audience.

I don't want to hinder you or restrict you from experimenting. On the contrary, I want to encourage it. But I also want to help you write good novels that will be publishable. So, my advice on experimenting with point of view is this: Tell a good story at the same time you're experimenting with point of view, and your story is more likely to succeed. Experiments in technique are interesting in an intellectual way, but to make them emotionally effective, in a way that excites your readers and not just literary critics or literary fiction authors, you need to wed your innovations to a splendid storyline. It's an even more powerful "experiment" to combine innovative techniques with good storytelling and character development.

FINAL WORDS ON CHALLENGING PERSPECTIVES

Obviously this chapter could not cover all of the challenging perspectives that exist out there or all of the possible ways an author could experiment with point of view. This chapter is simply meant as an introduction to these concepts. Once you've mastered the basics of point of view, I encourage you to experiment with point of view and to even try breaking the "rules" if your novel calls for it. After all, some of the most exciting writing in twentieth-century fiction has come about because authors broke the rules or conventions that were established in novel-writing up to that point.

It will be up to you, your work and your readers to decide whether your experiments or rule-breaking are effective in your novel. You will need to read novels that experiment with point of view in order to be aware of what's already been done; that way, you can do something groundbreaking and exciting in your own novel. Read and do the literary research, then go out there and tell a good story, but do it in a way that's never been done before.

EXERCISES FOR CHALLENGING PERSPECTIVES

1. Pick any mentally challenged or psychologically impaired group of people and, after you have spent a significant amount of time observing and researching them, write a scene from the perspective of a character who is challenged in the same way. Write the scene in first-person point of view. Make sure your vocabulary and sentence structure accurately reflect the thought processes of your mentally challenged or psychologically impaired narrator. Show the scene to your readers for their feedback and suggestions for improvement. Be sure to ask expert readers in the field to point out any vocabulary or sentence structure that such a psychologically impaired narrator would be incapable of using. Ask these expert readers for their suggestions on vocabulary replacements or revisions.

2. Write the scene from exercise 1 again, this time using unlimited point of view. Show the scene to your readers for their feedback and suggestions for improvement.

3. Write the scene from exercise 1 again, this time using outer limited point of view. That means you'll be restricted to showing only the external behavior of your mentally challenged or psychologically impaired character. You will stay out of the character's head. If there are other characters in the scene, you'll also stay out of their heads. You will have to describe behavior, including body language and nonverbals, that would indicate this character's state of mind and the other characters' reactions to him. Show the scene to your readers for their feedback and suggestions for improvement.

4. Write a scene in any point of view in which you reveal your character's nature by describing the objects in her room. Show the scene to your readers, and ask them what kind of person the character is. If they don't describe her as you would, ask your readers for their suggestions for improvement.

5. Write a scene in any point of view in which you reveal your character's nature by describing—in detail—his routines, his habits or customary practices. Show the scene to your readers and

ask them what kind of person the character is. If they don't describe him as you would, ask your readers for their suggestions for improvement.

6. Write a scene in first-person point of view that is narrated by an "I" or "we" who is telling the story, but try to attain the objectivity of outer limited point of view. In other words, try to blend first-person and outer limited points of view. Show this scene to your readers and ask them for their feedback and suggestions for improvement.

7. Write a scene in any point of view in which you describe a room your character is in when your character is drunk. No matter what point of view you write the scene in, make sure the objects you describe are the objects that would matter to a drunken character. Write the scene again, describing the same room when the character is happy. Write the scene again, each time giving the character different emotions so that different objects in the room matter to him. Make him grieving, blind, lonely, angry, bitter, pleased, triumphant, etc. Show the scenes to your readers to get their feedback and suggestions for improvement.

8. Write a five-paragraph scene in any point of view that reveals your character through her senses. For example, the first paragraph will deal with sight, so you'll only present what the character sees; the second paragraph will deal with hearing, so you will present everything the character hears; the third paragraph with taste; the fourth with smell; the last with touch. Show the scene to your readers to get their feedback and suggestions for improvement.

9. Write a scene in unlimited point of view in which "God" has a dementia. In other words, though God is omniscient and thus knows everything about all of His creation, He has become unreliable or can't remember everything that He knows. This may end up being something like the ambiguous unlimited point of view (discussed in detail in chapter 2); but then again, it may not. For feedback on this type of scene, you may need readers who are quite familiar with point of view. Get their feedback and suggestions for improvement.

NINE

MULTIPLE POINTS OF VIEW

A novelist can shift [point of view] if it comes off [successfully].

E.M. FORSTER

Aspects of the Novel

A novel written with multiple points of view contains completely different points of view in various sections. The author may combine first-person sections told by a narrator with unlimited sections written in the grammatical third person and allowing the author freedom of movement inside all her characters' heads. The author may combine first-person sections with second person, addressing the reader as "you," as many of the eighteenth- and nineteenth-century writers did. The second-person "you" might also be another character in the novel, an implied audience or humanity in general.

The author might use outer limited through much of the novel, but then switch to unlimited, as Hemingway often does; or she could use outer limited and switch occasionally to ambiguous unlimited, as Robbe-Grillet often does. Any time an author uses more than one point of view in the novel, she is using multiple points of view.

The specific combination of unlimited point of view used for the crime-fighting protagonists and inner limited point of view for the victims or the criminals has been recognized as a separate category by critics and become conventional in some crime novels. It is called combo point of view and is covered in chapter 7.

The novel with multiple points of view implies that the author consciously chose to change from point of view to another and not that the author accidentally lapsed from her chosen point of view.

(Lapses from point of view will be covered in this chapter, too.) When authors use multiple points of view, they have some artistic purpose for doing so.

MULTIPLE PERSPECTIVES VS. MULTIPLE POINTS OF VIEW

Multiple points of view should not be confused with multiple perspectives. In Faulkner's novel *The Sound and the Fury*, the author presents us with both multiple perspectives and multiple points of view. The first three sections of the book, all written in first-person point of view, give us three different perspectives—multiple perspectives—but do not give us multiple points of view. It is only because the last part of the novel is written in unlimited point of view that this book has multiple points of view. My first novel, *The Kommandant's Mistress*, presents both multiple perspectives and multiple points of view: The first two parts of the novel are different first-person narratives, providing the different perspectives, while the third part is written in ambiguous unlimited point of view, thus providing the multiple points of view.

My second novel, *Only With the Heart*, though it presents three different versions of the same story and thus gives multiple perspectives, is written entirely in first-person point of view. It does not have multiple points of view. Peter Straub's *Mr. X* and Jane Hamilton's *A Map of the World*, with their alternating first-person narratives, provide multiple perspectives but not multiple points of view.

TIP Multiple perspectives, several first-person narratives, for example, are not the same as multiple points of view. Multiple perspectives, however, no matter what point of view they're written in, can lend depth and richness to a novel.

MULTIPLE POINTS OF VIEW VS. UNLIMITED POINT OF VIEW

Writing a novel with multiple points of view is not the same as writing a novel in unlimited point of view. In unlimited point of view, the author, writing in the grammatical third person, moves freely inside and outside of the characters' head. Unlimited point of view is only one of the points of view available to an author. The novel with multiple points of view combines at least two different points of view, following the limitations or restrictions of each point of view in its own section.

ADVANTAGES OF USING
MULTIPLE POINTS OF VIEW

What would be the advantages to using multiple points of view in the same novel? That depends on the novel. Sometimes authors alternate between inner limited and first-person point of view to show a narrator's tenuous psychological state, as do Margaret Drabble in *The Waterfall* and Marguerite Duras in *The Lover*. In both cases the narrators of these novels talk about their own illicit sexual affairs in inner limited point of view rather than in first person, so the authors' shifting points of view adds psychological complexity and depth to the narrators.

Sometimes authors use multiple points of view to keep from revealing the criminal's identity, as do Tami Hoag in *A Thin Dark Line* and Karen Kijewski in *Stray Kat Waltz*. Both of these novels use first-person, inner limited and outer limited points of view throughout. In both of these novels, the use of inner limited point of view rather than first person when portraying the killer would have been more likely to reveal the identity of the killer since it would have revealed the gender of the killer. So the authors' use of first person, from the killer's perspective, keeps the killer's identity hidden from the readers for most of the book.

Sometimes authors writing crime or suspense fiction, which most frequently employs the combo point of view, add sections written in outer limited point of view to portray the objectivity of the legal system. Ed McBain does this in his novel *Kiss*. Most of the novel is in combo point of view, but when McBain adds the police interrogation transcripts, presented in outer limited point of view, he changes his novel from one written in combo point of view to one with multiple points of view.

Another advantage to using multiple points of view in the novel is its allowing the author to see the work in a new way (more on that in chapter 15 on revision).

THE DISADVANTAGE OF USING MULTIPLE POINTS OF VIEW

Some writers shift point of view constantly, sometimes in the middle of a sentence, as James Joyce does in *Ulysses*, but that doesn't mean it works for the readers. Most people, even those familiar with Joyce's work, are quite confused by rapidly shifting points of view. The biggest disadvantage of using multiple points of view in the novel is confusing your readers.

MULTIPLE POINTS OF VIEW IN LITERARY FICTION

There are many examples of literary fiction that provide both multiple perspectives and multiple points of view. Charles Dickens's *Bleak House*, my first novel *The Kommandant's Mistress* and Sir Walter Scott's *Redgauntlet* all combine first-person narratives with unlimited (or, as in my instance, ambiguous unlimited) point of view. Lawrence Durrell's masterpiece *The Alexandria Quartet* provides four different novels giving different perspectives on the same people and their behavior: *Justine*, *Balthazar* and *Clea* are all written in first person, while the third novel in the series, *Mountolive*, is written in unlimited point of view.

James Joyce's *Ulysses* moves from unlimited to first person and back to unlimited point of view, sometimes in the same sentence. Virginia Woolf combines several first-person sections with unlimited point of view in *The Waves*. Herman Melville's *Moby Dick* provides multiple perspectives in his first-person narratives as different characters reveal their thoughts, and he provides multiple points of view by writing in first person, unlimited and second person (for example, when the protagonist opens the novel with, "Call me Ishmael," he is addressing an implied audience).

Many of the literary novels that use multiple points of view have been discussed throughout this book and there are excerpts from many of them, such as Robbe-Grillet's *In the Labyrinth* and *Jealousy*, Fielding's *Tom Jones*, Nabokov's *Lolita*, Barthelme's *Snow White* and Robbins's *Even Cowgirls Get the Blues*.

MULTIPLE POINTS OF VIEW
IN COMMERCIAL FICTION

Despite myths to the contrary, multiple points of view have also been used quite successfully in commercial fiction. Michael Crichton combines first-person point of view in the form of e-mails and office memorandum with unlimited point of view in *Disclosure*. Anne Rice combines unlimited point of view with first person in *The Queen of the Damned*; Stephen King uses the same combination in *Gerald's Game*. Susan Krinard uses unlimited point of view and second person in *Once a Wolf*. There are also many examples of commercial fiction that provide multiple perspectives on the events in the novel.

TIP Novels with multiple points of view are not limited to literary fiction. If you'd like to write a commercial novel with multiple points of view, by all means, do so. But read literary and commercial novels containing multiple points of view before starting your own so that you can get a feel for what kind of multiple points of view will work for your novel.

USING MULTIPLE POINTS OF VIEW

Using multiple points of view in a novel is not the same as starting to write in one point of view and then switching the entire novel to another point of view, beginning in first person, for instance, and then changing the entire novel over to unlimited point of view. Using more than one point of view in a novel means that different sections are written in different points of view.

Should you use multiple points of view in your novel? That will depend on you and your novel. Are you trying to use more than one point of view just as an intellectual exercise or is something in the novel itself urging you to use multiple points of view? For example, are some of the characters insisting that they tell their own stories in their own words, necessitating a change for part of the novel from unlimited point of view to first person? When you do switch point of view, is it easier to write the scene or more difficult? If easier, it is an indication that the switch in point of view, thus providing multiple points of view, may be needed in the novel.

Are you using multiple points of view just because you want to or do you have some specific, artistic reason for it? Are you, for example, switching from unlimited point of view to inner limited when portraying the victim of a crime, as is done in the combo point of view in commercial crime fiction, so you can help your readers understand how professional crime-fighters solve crimes? You should know the answers to such questions if you write using multiple points of view.

There must be artistic reasons for using multiple points of view in your novel, or you will confuse your readers. However, you can learn to trust your intuition and your artistic subconscious in this area. If something is urging you to experiment with multiple points of view in your novel, then try it and see what happens. You will also have to find readers who understand the differences between points of view and get their feedback on the novel, specifically on the multiple points of view, before you send it out to agents and editors. Remember that multiple points of view, should you use them in your novel, should enhance the overall quality of the novel, adding depth and complexity to it.

How Often Should You Change Point of View?

The frequency with which you change point of view when using multiple points of view will depend on your novel itself, so there are no easy answers here. James Joyce, for example, sometimes changes point of view within the same sentence, and he is considered a great artist in English literature. Not many people are familiar with his work, however, so you could use James Joyce's novel *Ulysses* as a warning against changing too often and without alerting the readers.

You will have to get an intuitive feel for when to change point of view, and verify this with your readers, but I would suggest that changing every sentence is far too often. Changing every paragraph may be too often. Switching to another point of view in each chapter, perhaps alternating between first person and unlimited, for example, is not unreasonable and has been done with success in both literary and commercial fiction. As the excerpts from Margaret Drabble's novel *The Waterfall* (in chapter 8) and as Marguerite Duras's *The Lover* indicate, you can switch point of view in sections successfully, without even having formal chapter breaks. You will have to experiment and see what works best for you as an author, for each of your novels and for the readers who are giving you critical feedback.

TIP Use physical indicators to alert the readers to a change in point of view. Indicators used successfully by other published authors include additional spacing, asterisks, italics, change in font, separate chapters, chapter or section titles (with narrators' names, for example), etc.

Helping Your Readers When You Change Point of View

There are many physical ways to alert your readers that you are changing point of view. Some authors do it with additional spacing between sections, with asterisks, italics or a change in typeface (although the change in font has to be relatively dramatic for the reader to notice it). Some authors change chapters when changing point of view, even if the chapters are quite short. Some authors restrict their changing point of view to different sections of the novels, so the readers are more aware that the author is shifting points of view.

Remember that if your novel calls for multiple points of view, your goal is not to confuse and exasperate your readers. You want them to continue reading the novel and to feel that the book is enriched by the multiple points of view. If you were giving your readers instructions on how to get to a place they'd never been before, you wouldn't purposely give them incorrect directions or lead them into dead-end streets, and you should think of your novel in the same way. You are taking your readers to a new place, so you need to give them adequate and clear directions so they won't get lost. Therefore, you should use whatever physical indicators are necessary to make your multiple-points-of-view novel a pleasurable experience for your readers.

CHANGING POINT OF VIEW VS.
LAPSING FROM POINT OF VIEW

There is a difference from changing point of view and lapsing from the chosen point of view. If an author changes point of view, there should be a legitimate reason for doing so. It may be an artistic reason or it may have something to do with character development. In any event, most authors use physical indicators to avoid confusing their readers when they change point of view.

Lapsing from point of view implies that the author has made a mistake, that she has momentarily lapsed from the point of view she has chosen for the novel. Even great authors occasionally lapse from their point of view. F. Scott Fitzgerald is extremely inconsistent with point of view in his novel *Tender Is the Night*. In the story "Hills Like White Elephants," for example, which is written almost entirely in outer limited, Ernest Hemingway lapses. In this sentence—"He looked up the tracks but could not see the train"—Hemingway has lapsed from outer limited to unlimited point of view since outer limited is restricted to observable externals. If Hemingway had written, "There was no train," without telling us that the man couldn't see the train, it would have remained in outer limited point of view. By telling us, however, something that is internal to the man, Hemingway lapsed from his chosen point of view.

One of the most common areas for an author to lapse in point of view or perspective is when using first-person point of view. In William Faulkner's *The Sound and the Fury*, for example, Benjy sometimes uses vocabulary that he couldn't possibly understand since he is retarded to the age of three. Words like "rasped," "churned," "jolted" and "howled" indicate that Faulkner has lapsed from Benjy's perspective and from first-person point of view to unlimited.

One of the most common ways an author lapses from point of view in first person is when the author steps in to tell the readers of the book something that the narrator already knows and would not say, not even to herself, thus lapsing into unlimited point of view. When Patricia Cornwell's medical examiner-detective Kay Scarpetta is talking to the police detective Marino and one of them mentions "VICAP" and then Cornwell writes that VICAP is the

FBI's Violent Criminal Apprehension Program, she is lapsing from her first-person point of view. Scarpetta certainly knows what VI-CAP means, as does Marino. Clearly, Cornwell is writing that information for the reader, so she lapses from first person to move momentarily into unlimited point of view.

At other times in her novels, Cornwell consistently stays in first-person point of view, however, presenting unfamiliar terms and their definitions through dialogue that the characters would realistically not know. Here's an example of effectively defining terms while maintaining point of view, from chapter 13 of Cornwell's *Cause of Death*:

> Then the general said, "NAVSEA has been concerned about that shipyard for a while."
>
> "NAVSEA? What the hell is that?" Marino asked.
>
> "Naval Sea Systems Command," he said. "They're the people responsible for making certain that shipyards like the one in questions abide by the appropriate standards." ...
>
> "What is D-R-M-S out of Memphis?" I then asked.
>
> "Another fax number that Eddings called, as did you," he said. "Defense Reutilization Marketing Service. They handle all surplus sales, which must be approved by NAVSEA."

The VICAP information could also be presented in dialogue, although not with Marino or Scarpetta asking what it means, since they both know. But one of them could say, "I hate working with the FBI. The paperwork alone kills you, and how many violent criminals have they apprehended anyway?" or something along those lines so that the reader gets the necessary information without the author's lapsing from her point of view.

Once you set up a certain point of view for your novel, you must maintain it. If you change point of view, using multiple points of view, for specific artistic reasons, then of course it's permissible to change point of view. If you lapse from the novel's point of view, then you need to find a more appropriate way of handling the information presented in the lapse.

FINAL WORDS ON MULTIPLE POINTS OF VIEW

No matter what type of novel you want to write, you should not consider yourself prohibited from using multiple points of view, since there are examples in all genres that use more than one point of view. However, you should change point of view only if it adds psychological depth and complexity to your characters, offers multiple perspectives as well as multiple points of view and enhances your readers' understanding of the novel.

EXERCISE FOR MULTIPLE POINTS OF VIEW

This exercise has three different parts, each written in a different point of view, as detailed below.

Part I

Write any story in first-person point of view from the perspective of someone who has done or is about to do something that you yourself would never do. This narrator should be presented sympathetically, i.e., the readers must understand why he behaves as he does, even if they do not approve of or condone his behavior. You should have urgency in the first sentence, at the end of the first paragraph and periodically throughout part 1 (more on that in chapter 11). Remember that it is your obligation as the writer to keep the reader interested. Your narrator may be reliable or unreliable. Put conflict in the story, and include a climax. Concentrate on developing round characters, even if they are minor characters. If you have dialogue, use realistic-sounding dialogue that shows conflict, the history or relationship of the characters, and the nature of the characters. Use urgency, simile, metaphor, and allusion to make your story and characters come alive for the reader.

Part 2

Rewrite the same story from part 1, this time changing both point of view and perspective: Write in inner limited point of view from the perspective of the person who has been or will be harmed by the action of the person in part 1. This character must also be presented sympathetically. You should have urgency in the first sentence, at the end of the first paragraph and periodically throughout part 2. Concentrate on developing round characters, even if they are minor characters. If you have dialogue, use realistic-sounding dialogue that shows conflict, the history or relationship of the characters, and the nature of the characters. Use urgency, simile, metaphor, and allusion to make your story and characters come alive for the reader.

Part 3

Write the same story again, once again changing point of view. This time use outer limited point of view, presenting the characters and events from parts 1 and 2 but in an objective, nonjudgmental way. Both characters who appear in parts 1 and 2 must appear equally sympathetically in this third section. You should have urgency in the first sentence, at the end of the first paragraph and periodically throughout part 3. In this point of view, you do not reveal characters' thoughts, desires, feelings or motivations unless the characters themselves speak these things aloud. You may only report what you can see or hear. Remember that you, as the author, are the fly on the wall. There is no narrator in this part. There should be conflict in the story and a climax.

Show this exercise to your readers for their feedback and suggestions for improvement.

TEN

VOICE AND ARTISTIC INTUITION

> Anyone can write when the ideas are flowing
> and the characters are behaving.
>
> DONNA LEVIN
>
> *Get That Novel Started!*

The largest hurdles to overcome in your attempt to master point of view will be to learn when you are writing as yourself—in your own voice—and when you are writing in a character's voice, to learn when you are being objective and when you're being subjective, to learn when you're passing judgment on your characters through your word choices and when you're not. Once you've mastered these things, which basically means mastering point of view, you will be able to master voice and will be able to experiment more confidently with various points of view for your novels. These things take practice, but they also mean learning to trust your intuition. This chapter includes many exercises, therefore, that are designed to help you learn to access and honor your artistic intuition.

Many of these exercises have a meditation aspect to quiet your conscious mind and give you access to your subconscious, creative mind. If you've never done this kind of thing before, you may find it weird or intimidating. Even if you find these exercises too mystical, metaphysical, spiritual or downright spooky for your taste, I urge you to try at least one of them. No matter what point of view you write in, your novel will improve if you learn to listen to your artistic intuition. None of these exercises will hurt your writing in any way. In fact, because they help quiet your conscious mind and put you in direct contact with your subconscious, creative mind, they can only improve your writing.

VOICE AND THE NOVEL

"Voice" in fiction is an extremely complicated concept because it is not as easily identified as plot or symbolism, for example. Johnny Payne, in his book *Voice and Style*, writes that there is a "common misperception [that] voice for an author [is] what 'screen presence' is to an actor—some mysterious quality that you either have or you don't." Though it's difficult to master voice, it's not hard to understand it.

Just What Is Voice Anyway?

Think of voice in fiction, literally, as a voice. When your close friends, loved ones or children call you on the phone, you recognize their voices: Their accents, timbre, vocabulary, intonation patterns and sentence structure all combine to give them unique voices that you have learned to recognize without their having to identify themselves by name. This same thing can be true of both authors and literary characters.

Characters' Voices

Vocabulary, idiom, sentence structure, etc., can all combine in a way that is unique to a fictional narrator, giving that narrator a voice unlike any other character's. For instance, Mark Twain's Huck in *The Adventures of Huckleberry Finn* has a unique voice, as does Kaye Gibbons's Ellen Foster in the novel by the same name, Harper Lee's Scout in *To Kill a Mockingbird* and Roddy Doyle's Paddy in *Paddy Clarke Ha Ha Ha*. The voice of the character is integrally bound with personality so that readers always associate the voice with that character. This is a good thing since it makes the character more memorable.

Authors' Voices

An author, too, can have a voice, comprised of elements like sentence structure, writing style and vocabulary, which identify passages in her work to the readers just as if they were hearing a loved one on the telephone. William Faulkner, James Joyce and Ernest Hemingway are just a few of the authors whose work is distinguished by their voice. Readers can recognize a passage written by Hemingway even without his name on it because it has Hemingway's unique voice. (Of course, having such a unique voice can also open an author up to criticism and parody, as happens annually in the "Best of the Worst Hemingway" contest, where authors imitate Hemingway's voice at his worst.)

How Do You Learn Voice?

While it is true that voice can be learned, many writers do not do so because learning to have a distinct voice in fiction means mastering all the other elements of fiction writing, but especially point of view. To put it most simply, a mastery of voice comes after a mastery of point of view. The author then must develop an awareness for language and what makes each person's language unique and memorable, putting this knowledge into her novels so that her readers can recognize her writing simply by her voice.

Authors and Their Own Voices

Most authors write in their own voices. Every book they write sounds exactly like every other book they write, and if you were to talk to the author, you would find that his books sound like he does. Now if this is what the author intends, then that is good. If the author wishes to expand his writing repertoire and learn to write in different voices, however, he will have to learn how to use different points of view and to successfully create realistic characters and tell good stories in all points of view.

First-Person Point of View and Voice

Some beginning writers operate under the assumption that if they're writing in first-person point of view, then the voice of the character is automatically unique. Often they will have novels with more than one first-person narrative, providing multiple perspectives on the novel's action but with all the voices of these different narratives identical. If the similarity in voice in these first-person narratives is intentional and symbolic, as it was in my first novel *The Kommandant's Mistress*, where the similarity in the protagonists' voices is symbolic of the brutality each undergoes in the concentration camp despite their differing roles as perpetrator and victim, then having similar voices for different first-person narratives is appropriate. If this similarity is unintentional, however, then the author needs to work on mastering first-person point of view and allow each character's individual voice to come through.

In first-person point of view, especially, listening to your intuition is extremely important in order to present a character's voice that is not simply your own voice disguised as your narrator's voice. The most challenging aspect of writing a novel is creating a voice that is unique to you as an author and to your characters. Mastering first-person point of view does not mean simply writing using "I" or "we." It means learning to hear the narrator's unique voice and learning to differentiate it from your own.

TIP Don't consciously worry too much about developing a unique voice until you've mastered the remaining elements for good fiction writing, including using different points of view.

Which Is It: Author's Voice or Narrator's Voice?

When your readers critique your manuscript for you, do they believe that everything you write is your own personal belief? If they do, then this may be an indication that you are writing everything in your own personal voice. If your readers are able to discuss the ideas in the novel and recognize that they are the narrator's ideas or beliefs rather than your own personal beliefs, this is a sign that you have differentiated between the character's voice and your own. For example, in my first novel, *The Kommandant's Mistress*, which is narrated in part by the Nazi Kommandant of a concentration camp, no readers assumed that I had been a Nazi myself. It was clear to them that it was the Kommandant's voice they were hearing and not my own.

Steps Toward Voice

Learning to hear the difference between your voice and those of your characters takes practice, but it can be done. Becoming aware of voice as a concept is one step; reading novels and authors known for their distinctive voices is another, as is listening to your own artistic intuition, which you can learn by doing some of the exercises at the end of this chapter.

INTUITION AND POINT OF VIEW

In order to master point of view, you will have to practice writing in various points of view and also learn how to trust your artistic intuition.

Artistic Intuition

Artistic intuition, which some call "instinct," is not a logical, mental process but rather a "feeling" that things should be done in a certain way to be most effective for the novel and its audience. When an author wakes up in the middle of the night with an idea for a brilliant scene, that is artistic intuition at work. When a character "misbehaves" and does something the author hadn't included in his outline, that is artistic intuition trying to guide the author in writing the novel.

An author inexperienced with listening to his intuition often discounts such feelings because he doesn't have enough writing experience to realize that his intuition is guiding him toward the best form for his novel. Because he doesn't consciously know what the best form for the novel is, he doesn't listen to his own intuition. At conferences and workshops, when I'm critiquing manuscripts and suggest some deletions, beginning writers often look at me in surprise and say, "I wondered if I should take that scene out." If you wonder if you should take a scene out (or put one in, for that matter), then do so. That's your artistic intuition trying to talk to you.

But What Does This Have to Do With Point of View?

Point of view, more than any other aspect of creative writing, requires an author to be in touch with his artistic intuition in order to attain mastery. An author can practice writing in different points of view endlessly, but until he also learns to listen to his artistic intuition, he'll never be able to determine when a particular point of view is working successfully or which point of view would be most effective for his novel. Furthermore, if an author does not learn to listen to his artistic intuition, it will never become easier for him to write in different points of view because the choice of point of view is not always a logical, rational choice; rather, it often depends on the author's feeling that a particular point of view is working for that novel.

All writers can gain access to their artistic intuition or feeling about their novels. Practice, patience and learning to listen to what your feelings are telling you will help you successfully tune in to your artistic intuition. The more in touch you are with your intuition and your creative subconscious, the quicker you'll be able to master point of view.

Tuning in to Your Intuition

There are quite a few ways to develop your intuition for writing purposes. Becoming almost hyperconscious of the writing process itself will allow you direct access to the creative subconscious. Doing creative writing exercises unrelated to the novel you're working on will also develop your intuition, as will meditating, which quiets the conscious mind and allows you to hear the subconscious one.

Becoming Aware of Your Writing Process

To develop your artistic intuition, you need to become more aware of the writing process itself. One of the ways to do this is to make notes about writing the novel while you are doing it, for example, at the end of each writing session. Did you find it easier to develop the character in first-person point of view than in unlimited, for example? Do you work most comfortably in unlimited point of view? Do you prefer first person over inner limited point of view since first person offers greater intimacy and emotional bonding? When you revise, does it help you to change point of view? Many of the creative writing processes are guided by artistic intuition, so making yourself aware of the processes gives you greater access to your intuition. If you keep notes on the writing process itself, you will benefit from them when you write future novels and when you're trying to master different points of view.

Creative Writing Exercises

To develop your artistic intuition, it is helpful to keep a creative writing journal for exercises or spontaneous writing. Every day when you first wake up or before you begin working on your novel, you should do at least one exercise in your journal. You can do some of the exercises in this book or exercises found in other creative writing books such as Natalie Goldberg's *Writing Down the Bones* and *Wild Mind*, Robin Hemley's *Turning Life Into Fiction,*

Julia Cameron's *The Artist's Way* and *The Vein of Gold* or Story Press Editors' *Idea Catcher*. All of these creative writing exercises, because they push you in directions you may not have thought of on your own, will help open up your artistic intuition.

Unclutter Your Conscious Mind

Even more important than becoming aware of the writing process or doing specific creative writing exercises, however, is uncluttering your conscious mind so that you can more immediately access your subconscious creative mind. This might include meditation, walking or other exercising, sitting quietly, or writing in your journal for at least ten to fifteen minutes—not on any particular topic—simply to clear your mind. You might also try focused free-writing, when you write for ten to fifteen minutes but on a particular topic.

Many of the exercises at the end of this chapter encourage you to meditate as a way to access your creative intuition. There are many writers who regularly do this, and there are many fine books out there that you can use to unclutter your conscious mind in order to reach your subconscious, creative mind. Natalie Goldberg's books help you do it specifically connected with writing, as do Julia Cameron's. Books and tapes designed specifically to increase your awareness or teach you to meditate, such as those by Jon Kabat-Zinn (*Wherever You Go There You Are*) or Jack Kornfield (*A Path With Heart* and *Meditation for Beginners* [tape]) will also be quite helpful in allowing you to quiet your mind so you can listen to your artistic intuition.

Final Words on Intuition and Point of View

Once you begin to listen to your artistic intuition and honor it by acting on your feelings—for example, by cutting scenes you feel should be cut or switching from unlimited to first-person point of view—you will find that your intuition will be much more likely to talk to you and to talk louder. This will be especially helpful when you're working on point of view because point of view decisions, for many writers, are often intuitive ones. Therefore, the more you listen to your artistic intuition, the better your writing will be and the quicker you'll master point of view.

EXERCISES FOR TUNING IN TO YOUR INTUITION

1. Sit very still in a comfortable position, in a quiet room, where you will not be interrupted and where there are no distractions such as the television, telephone, etc. Close your eyes. Concentrate on your breathing for a few minutes. Notice how the breath goes in and out. Notice your body's movements during the breath cycle. If it helps you to quiet your conscious mind to mentally say "in" with each inhalation and "out" with each exhalation, then do so. Try to do this for at least ten minutes, twice a day. If you can also do it before you start writing for the day, then do so.

After you have quieted your mind, you might ask your intuition a question regarding your novel, for example, "What point of view will work best?" or "What happens next in the novel's plot?" Then return your concentration to your breathing and wait for the answer. And you must wait for the answer. It may take a few minutes, a few hours, a few days to get a response. Of course, if the answer doesn't come after ten minutes or so, you don't have to sit still this entire time; you can go about the daily business of life or continue working on other parts of the novel. Simply being aware that you are waiting for an answer will allow your intuition to speak to you. Your answer may come in the form of an image, so that you may "see" your novel written in unlimited point of view or "see" the next development in the plot's action. Trust your intuition to know the answer. If no answer comes before your next meditation session, ask it again.

2. Write for at least ten minutes about something that you are trying to work out in the novel. This might be something having to do with your character's history, with the character's voice, with the action, etc. For the entire ten minutes, write only about the problem you're working on. If you normally write in longhand, then write in longhand. If you normally work directly at the computer, then do this exercise on the keyboard. The goal in this exercise is to access the creative subconscious and artistic intuition by making yourself aware of the problem you're trying to solve and by performing the same task as when you're writing: moving the pen on paper or typing at the computer. After you've written for at least ten minutes without stopping, you should feel calmer and have more access to your intuition, even if you don't know the answer to the original problem.

EXERCISES FOR USING INTUITION
TO LISTEN TO YOUR CHARACTERS

1. Prepare yourself by meditating, following the instructions for the first "tuning into your intuition" exercise in this chapter. After you have done that, ask your character a question that will reveal her history to you. For example, why did that character marry another one? What attracted her to her husband (or vice versa)? Ask your character the question and then return your attention to your breathing as you wait for the answer. If the answer doesn't come in a few minutes, simply acknowledge that you're waiting for the answer and then go about your business. You can work on your novel, but don't work on the section that needs that answer before you write it. Don't rush the answer. When it comes to you, you'll know.

2. Alternatively, do this meditation exercise before you go for a walk (or run). Walk a little while to quiet your mind and access your subconscious, then ask the question and wait for the answer as you continue to walk. Don't force the answer. It will come when your character is ready to release the information. Until then, respect your character, be patient and work on other sections of the novel (or on other novels, if necessary).

3. Sit quietly in one of the rooms of your house. Close your eyes. Breathe deeply and concentrate on your breathing. Think of your character. Try to feel the character inside your own body. Let the character expand until she is completely inside you. Now open your eyes and look at the room through your character's eyes. What does she notice? What does she pay attention to? Ask her why she notices particular items. Wait for her answer. Do not judge your character's responses. You are there to witness. Be objective. Learn to listen to your character. Write it down or speak it into your tape recorder after you have spent enough time listening to your character.

4. Go to the woods, the lake, your backyard—anyplace in nature. Sit quietly. Close your eyes. Continue all the steps in the previous exercise. Look at the landscape through your character's eyes. What does she notice? What does she pay attention to? Ask her why she notices particular items. Wait for her answer. Do not judge your character's responses. Be an objective witness. Learn to listen to your character. Write it down or speak it into your tape recorder after you have spent enough time listening to your character.

ELEVEN

URGENCY AND POINT OF VIEW

Point of view is the most complex element of fiction.
JANET BURROWAY
Writing Fiction: A Guide to Narrative Craft

If I hadn't fallen off the mountain, I never would have believed it. Actually, I did believe it before I fell off the mountain, but the first sentence of this paragraph is an example of the most important element of fiction today—even more important than point of view—urgency. Writers need urgency in their fiction in order to have vibrant, intriguing, publishable fiction.

WHAT IS URGENCY?

Urgency is what keeps the reader reading. It's that simple. Urgency is whatever elements in the book make the reader want to continue turning the pages.

WHY URGENCY?

Writers are competing with television, videos, movies and other authors for their audiences, so contemporary writers have a more challenging task than their predecessors did. Urgency should not be "pasted on" or simply attached to the piece of writing. It must be an integral part of it, inseparable from the plot's conflict, character development or characters' voices. This urgency will keep the readers clamoring for more, so it must be honest urgency, that is, it must naturally evolve from the characters, the plot and the circumstances of the novel you are writing. Read the opening of contemporary novels, and you'll find some wonderful examples of urgency.

- When I was little I would think of ways to kill my daddy. (Kaye Gibbons, *Ellen Foster*)
- Mr. and Mrs. Dursley, of number four, Privet Drive, were proud to say that they were perfectly normal, thank you very much. (J.K. Rowling, *Harry Potter and the Sorcerer's Stone*)
- They shoot the white girl first. (Toni Morrison, *Paradise*)

URGENCY IS NOT A NEW CONCEPT

Though it may have been called suspense, mystery or intrigue, urgency is present is most of the enduring literary works, no matter how long ago they were written. Shakespeare's *Hamlet* begins with the guards discussing the ghost who looks like Hamlet's dead father and who appears even as the guards are talking about him. Urgency has always been present in the best literature, no matter its point of view or genre. Though some published authors may relax once they have established audiences and no longer include urgency, new writers cannot afford to do so.

TYPES OF URGENCY

There are some basic areas you can include urgency in your novel; these are in plot, character development and voice.

Urgency and Plot

Urgency is easiest to develop when it is part of the plot because you need conflict in plot, and conflict lends itself easily to urgency. The traditional divisions of conflict are these:

- man vs. man
- man vs. himself
- man vs. nature
- man vs. supernatural

Plot urgency is relatively similar no matter what point of view you choose to write in; you simply have to tell a good story, one whose events will keep your readers' attention. First person, inner limited, second person, unlimited, combo, multiple—all these points of view can easily encompass plot urgency and conflict. No matter which point of view you choose, you should increase the conflicts in importance and intensity throughout the novel to maintain your readers' interest.

Plot urgency in outer limited point of view is absolutely essential. In this point of view, the only thing the readers can know about the characters is their behavior and dialogue. Therefore, it is imperative that your characters do or say things that will keep the readers turning the pages. Since you, as the author, are also limited to presenting only the external behaviors of your characters, you can master this point of view more effectively with plot urgency and conflict. You will have concrete actions and behaviors to present to your readers.

The only conflict you cannot easily present in outer limited point of view is Man vs. himself, unless, of course, you present the character's internal conflict in external ways. You cannot show a character arguing with himself, for example, unless he does it aloud. Since you cannot show any characters' inner emotional or psychological life in this point of view, you will have to work harder to show the inner conflict in an external manner. Read Alain Robbe-Grillet's *Jealousy* for excellent examples of presenting plot urgency in outer limited point of view.

Urgency and Character Development

Urgency in character development can be integrally related to point of view. Character development urgency is most challenging in unlimited point of view since the author can provide the readers with any and all interpretations of the characters and their actions, thus leaving nothing for the readers to explore. Still, as I explained in chapter 2, there is a difference between an author's *knowing* everything and *revealing* everything about his characters. That means you can put sufficient character development urgency in unlimited point of view by not revealing everything about the characters to the readers from the very beginning.

In first-person and inner limited points of view, the readers are restricted to viewing the world from one character's perspective. Since only this character's emotions, thoughts and motivations will be revealed to the readers, these points of view automatically set up urgency in character development, both for the characters through whose perspective we view the action and for the other characters in the novel, all of whom are presented externally. Whatever the protagonist does not know about other characters in the novel in these points of view, for instance, the readers cannot know. That creates character development urgency.

Outer limited point of view creates the greatest opportunity for character development urgency since the author is not revealing any interior or hidden motives. Because only the external life of all the characters is presented, readers are greatly involved in figuring out the causes for the characters' behavior. Unless you present the character's secret desires and ulterior motives in a spoken monologue, as is done in theater, for example, the readers will not know why the character is behaving in a certain way. That creates character development urgency because the readers will want to continue reading the novel to understand the character.

Unfortunately, outer limited point of view also has the greatest chance of alienating readers for the very reason it can be most interesting to the author. Since readers must figure out everything about the characters' inner lives for themselves, based on the author's depiction of the characters' external behavior, the readers may get frustrated or may misinterpret the characters' behavior. Outer limited point of view is always extremely challenging to an author, but revealing character development urgency in this point of view is very demanding.

Urgency and Voice

A distinctive or unusual voice, whether a narrator's or an author's, usually doesn't appear until the author has mastered point of view (read more on voice in chapter 10). However, you can understand the concept without being proficient at creating it. When the voice in a piece of literature has urgency, it is the voice itself that makes the audience want to continue reading. Zora Neale Hurston's "How It Feels to Be Colored Me" is an example of wonderful urgency in voice, as is the opening of Dostoevsky's *Notes from the Underground* (see chapter 8 for an excerpt) and Melville's *Moby Dick*, all of which happen to be in first-person point of view.

Urgency in voice is directly related to point of view, and many writers find it easier to have urgency in voice when writing in first-person point of view. This ease may be due to the intimate bond created when readers hear the narrator's words. However, it is also possible to have voice urgency in other points of view, as Hemingway's novels demonstrate. In unlimited or outer limited points of view, it is the author's distinctive voice that creates the urgency rather than a narrator's.

MAINTAINING URGENCY

Urgency must be maintained throughout the piece of fiction to be effective. Chapter 2 of Leo Tolstoy's *The Death of Iván Ilých*, for example, begins with this line: Iván Ilých's life had been most simple and most ordinary and therefore most terrible." That's fantastic urgency and it's in unlimited point of view. Though it may seem artificial for you to continually have to be aware of urgency as you're writing the novel, it will not be artificial to your audience. On the contrary, even when an experienced writer reads other books with urgency, the writer is still turning the pages as rapidly as he can to figure out what's going to happen, just as any other readers would. As you make the urgency integral to the plot, character development or voice, you can write in any point of view and effectively maintain your readers' interest.

TIP Master urgency before you attempt to conquer point of view. Urgency is one of the keys to writing a good novel. Once you've mastered that, it will be easier to tackle point of view.

HOW OFTEN SHOULD YOU INCLUDE URGENCY?

The most important thing to remember in creating urgency, no matter what point of view you're writing your novel in, is that any place you might lose the reader's attention is a place you need to have urgency. Here are my suggestions for urgency placement:

- the first sentence
- the last sentence of the first paragraph
- at the beginning and end of each chapter
- at the beginning and end of each section, if your novel is divided into sections
- any time you change narrators or points of view (these could be considered informal section divisions, so you should have urgency at the beginning and end of each, even if the section division is not formal)
- periodically throughout the novel

EXERCISES TO DEVELOP URGENCY
AND POINT OF VIEW

1. Write the first sentence of your novel and make sure it has urgency, whether in plot, character development or in voice, using first-person point of view. Pretend this is the only sentence your audience will read, that they'll buy the book based on how intriguing or interesting they find this first sentence. Make it the best piece of writing you can. Now, show it to as many other people as you can and ask them these questions:

- Would they want to continue reading based on the first sentence alone? If so, then you do have urgency. If not, you need to work on it.
- Would they want to buy the book in paperback based on the first sentence alone? If so, then you have good urgency.
- Would they want to buy the book in hardcover based on the first sentence alone? If so, then you have excellent urgency.
- Would they want to buy the book in hardcover or paperback and every other book you've written based on the first sentence alone? If so, then you have fantastic urgency, and you've definitely mastered this concept.

2. Write the first sentence of your novel and make sure it has urgency, whether in plot, character development or in voice, using unlimited point of view. Remember that your audience will buy the book based on how intriguing or interesting they find this first sentence. Make it the best piece of writing you can.

3. Now, write the first sentence of your novel with urgency using inner limited point of view. Follow the same procedure that you have for the other exercises.

4. Write another first sentence with urgency using outer limited point of view. Follow the same procedure that you have for the other exercises.

5. Examine all the opening sentences that you have written with urgency. Which of the opening sentences do you find most comfortable to write, first person, unlimited, outer limited or inner limited? Do you find it easier to put urgency in any particular point of view? If you find it more difficult to write in one particular point of view, it may be that you need to develop your skill in this area. Often writers get used to a certain point of view and find it difficult

to write well in the other points of view. Use this exercise to develop urgency in all the points of view.

6. Write the opening paragraph for each of the first sentences you've written, paying particular attention to which of the points of view is more challenging or easier to develop urgency in. Use this exercise to develop urgency in all the points of view.

TWELVE

CHARACTER DEVELOPMENT AND POINT OF VIEW

Point of view is a less obvious, and less glamorous, element of a novel than character or plot. No one ever recommends a book to you exclaiming, "Man, the point of view will blow you away!" Nor can I recall ever seeing a jacket blurb that praised the author, "We always know whose head we're in."

DONNA LEVIN

Get That Novel Written!

Character development is one of the most important things an author has to master to create memorable and vivid fiction. Without realistic characters, the reader will not be able to relate emotionally to the novel. Also, unless you have realistic characters, it will be more difficult to master point of view, especially first-person point of view.

TRADITIONAL CATEGORIES OF CHARACTERS

When being discussed in literature and in creative writing classes, characters have typically been divided into four major types or categories: flat, round, static and evolving.

Flat Characters

Flat characters are like cartoons or caricatures: They are one-dimensional; they are not realistic human beings because they lack the emotional depth and complexity of living humans. Flat characters often become stereotypes whose behavior is predictable according to their types.

If you are writing in first-person point of view, it would be difficult to make the narrator a flat character since we are viewing the world from inside his head. That vantage point virtually guarantees that he'll be a round character. The biggest danger in this instance would be that all the minor characters end up flat, especially if the narrator concentrates only on himself and his emotions. Unlimited point of view can often create flat characters if the author provides all moral judgment for his readers—making the hero perfect and the villain dreadful, for example—so if you're using that point of view, you must be especially careful not to create flat characters.

Round Characters

Unlike flat characters, round characters, as their name implies, are three-dimensional. In other words, they are realistic human characters with the emotional range, depth and complexity that real people have. Most famous characters in classic literature are round characters. If you find yourself questioning a character's motives or behavior, then in all likelihood, that character is a round one.

It is relatively easy to create round characters in first-person or inner limited point of view because you are viewing the events in the novel from the character's perspective. As long as you are aware of the difference between round and flat characters, it should also be easy for you to create round characters in unlimited point of view.

Second-person point of view involves some difficulty in creating round characters because of the various persons the "you" can be referring to. As the author, you must be clear on the identity of the "you" when using second person and develop that "you" as a character, even if he does not actually appear in the work or if you are directly addressing your readers. That way, the "you" will become a character for your readers.

Outer limited point of view presents the most difficulties and challenges for creating round characters because you must stay out of all the characters' heads. Because no inner lives or unspoken motivations are revealed, it is extremely hard to present fully human, complex characters in this point of view. If you are willing to accept the challenge, however, you can stretch your skills as a writer by trying to create round characters in outer limited point of view.

Static and Evolving Characters

Often people confuse static characters, who do not change through-out the piece of literature, with flat characters, who are not realistic human beings. Round characters can be static. Their being static simply means that they do not change throughout the work.

If they do not change and they are round characters, then the author obviously has a reason for that character's not changing. It may be political commentary, symbolism, irony, etc. The Kommandant in my first novel, *The Kommandant's Mistress*, for example, is a static round character. Though he is a complex, fully developed human being, he does not change during the course of the work. Because he does not come to grips with the moral issues in his life (specifically, with what the Nazis did to the Jews during the Holocaust) and because he does not grow morally, he remains a static character though he is a round one. He symbolically represents any humans who cling to oppressive ideologies.

Evolving characters, as their name indicates, change through the course of a work. A flat character, since it is not like a real human being, would not be able to be an evolving character. His changing would automatically elevate him into a round character. Melville's narrator Ishmael changes during his journey with Captain Ahab, so Ishmael is an evolving character. In commercial fiction, the characters may evolve over a series of novels, such as Robert A. Heinlein's Lazarus Long, who appears in several different works, including *Time Enough for Love* and *Methuselah's Children*.

First-person, inner limited and unlimited points of view lend themselves readily to the creation of evolving characters. Second person and outer limited, for the reasons listed previously under "Round Characters," present more challenges to an author when trying to create evolving characters in these points of view.

CHARACTER DEVELOPMENT IN LITERARY VS. COMMERCIAL FICTION

In literary fiction, no matter what its point of view, characters are presented complete within whatever novel they appear. Thus, all round characters are realistic human beings in that novel. A reader does not have to read other books by that author to find out more about the characters introduced in one particular book.

In commercial fiction, however, especially in novels written in series such as mystery, science fiction or detective novels, the character development often takes place over the series. Therefore, if a reader looks at only one novel out of the series, the characters may appear to be flat or static or both. Reading multiple books in the series will reveal the character development, so that the character may be round and evolving over the course of several books. This would be true no matter what point of view the author has chosen for his series.

IMPLIED CHARACTERS

At times, a novel will have implied characters, that is, characters who are either not present in the work or who are present only through their voices. Second-person point of view is used for addressing implied characters. The other characters in the novel may simply talk directly to these implied characters, as Nabokov's narrator does when he addresses the "ladies and gentlemen of the jury" in *Lolita*. The other characters may actually interact with these implied characters, as Max does in my novel *The Kommandant's Mistress*, when the implied characters are his captors after the war, though Max never tells the reader directly to whom he is speaking.

The implied character might also be a fictional biographer, diarist or letter writer. The implied character's voice may give the readers all the information they need to know about that character, as does Dr. Daniels's voice in my second novel *Only With the Heart*.

Implied characters should be as fully developed as characters who are actually present in the novel. Use hints about their history to make them come alive for the readers. Again, this will be most difficult in outer limited point of view.

CREATING REALISTIC CHARACTERS

Even if you are writing commercial fiction and intend to write a series of novels containing the same characters, it is advisable to develop the characters as fully as possible within each novel in the series. In literary fiction, of course, it is essential that the characters come to life in that one book. Although it takes patience and practice, it is not difficult to create realistic, round characters with the depth and complexity of living human beings, no matter what point of view your novel is written in. Here are some brief guidelines to help you.

Guidelines for Creating Realistic Characters
- Like your characters.
- Let them live their own lives.
- Know every character's past.
- Give each character both positive and negative traits.
- Use unreliability, denial and positive illusions to create psychological realism and complexity.

FINAL WORDS ON CREATING REALISTIC CHARACTERS

Liking your characters, allowing them to live their own lives, endowing them with good and bad characteristics, the skillful use of unreliable narrators—these are all valuable tools for creating realistic characters in any point of view. Observing human nature and becoming conscious of the techniques other skillful writers use will also help you develop your own characters, especially if you become aware of the techniques authors use in different points of view.

TIP If your readers talk about your characters as if they were real people, e.g., asking things like, "Why on earth doesn't Bill leave Marion?" then that's an indication that you've created realistic, round characters who have psychological depth and complexity.

EXERCISES FOR REALISTIC CHARACTERS AND POINT OF VIEW

1. Pick any historical, biblical or literary character renowned for doing evil: Satan, Iago, Delilah, Stalin, Lizzie Borden, Jeffrey Dahmer, Nero all work well for this exercise. Write a scene with

urgency in unlimited point of view that shows something good about that character that the character would not necessarily want others to know. Do not tell the readers who the narrator is. Give enough details in the text so that the readers would recognize the narrator. Present the character so that the readers gain a new appreciation and understanding for that figure. In other words, give the demon a human face. Show it to your readers, and ask for their reactions and suggestions for improvement.

2. Pick any historical, biblical or literary character renowned for doing good: Jesus, Mother Theresa, Buddha, Moses, Ghandi, Hercules, George Washington, Martin Luther King, Jr., all work well for this exercise. Write a scene with urgency in unlimited point of view that shows something unsavory or bad about that character that the character would not necessarily want others to know. Present the character so that the readers gain a new appreciation and understanding for that figure. In other words, tarnish the halo. Show it to your readers and ask for their reactions and suggestions for improvement.

3. Write any of the above exercises using first-person point of view, that is, so that the character is narrating the scene himself. Then ask yourself the following questions:

- Do you find it easier to create a sympathetic portrait of a villain in first-person point of view? In unlimited point of view? Why?
- Do you find it easier to create an unsympathetic portrait of a hero in first-person point of view? In unlimited point of view? Why?
- Show the scenes to your readers. Do they feel more or less sympathy for the character depending on point of view? If so, why?
- Is it easier for you to create more sympathy for a character in first person than in unlimited?
- Is it easier for you to create more antipathy for a character in first person than in unlimited?

Bear in mind that there are no right or wrong answers to these questions. The point of all these exercises is to help you become a better writer and to assist you in mastering point of view. If you find it easier to create sympathetic characters in first-person point of view, for example, then that would indicate that you are more comfortable working in that point of view, that you have more experience in it, that you might like to do your novel in that point of view, that you should spend more time working on the other points of view since you have a writing weakness in that area, etc. The goal of this book is to help you get more comfortable and proficient in all areas of novel writing and in all points of view.

4. Try the above exercises in outer limited point of view. This will probably be the most challenging exercise because you will not present any of the character's thoughts, feelings and motivations unless they are spoken aloud. Present only what you can observe or hear. Show behavior and report dialogue, if any. Do not judge the character. Try to present his actions as unemotionally and as nonjudgmentally as possible. Show it to your readers and ask for their reactions and suggestions for improvement.

THIRTEEN

SETTING, DIALOGUE AND POINT OF VIEW

When you change point of view, you change the story.

ROBIN HEMLEY

Turning Life Into Fiction

Urgency and realistic characters are among the most challenging things novelists have to deal with. They are also intimately connected with point of view. Other elements of the novel, such as setting and dialogue, may not seem as closely connected with point of view, but they are because point of view can determine which setting details you include and how the dialogue is presented.

SETTING AND POINT OF VIEW

Setting is more than just the physical description of the landscape or the locale against which the action of the novel takes place. Setting also includes the atmosphere of the piece, such as the brooding and foreboding atmosphere of gothic or horror novels, the costume of the characters and the time period in which the novel takes place. The intellectual, moral, religious and social conditions of the novel are also considered part of the setting, as are the characters' occupations and daily manner of living.

Unlimited Point of View and Setting

Describing setting is easiest in unlimited point of view because, as its name suggests, you are not limited in any way in your presentation. Take a look at the opening of chapter 2 of Thomas Hardy's *Tess of the D'Urbervilles*, written in unlimited point of view.

> The village of Marlott lay amid the north-eastern undula-
> tions of the beautiful Vale of Blakemore or Blackmoor
> aforesaid—an engirdled and secluded region, for the most
> part untrodden as yet by tourist or landscape-painter,
> though within a four hours' journey from London.

Hardy then proceeds to give us some of the historical information about the region, something that is easier and more natural in
unlimited point of view than in any of the other points of view
(unless your narrator is a history buff and has some justifiable
reason in the novel for presenting this kind of information).

Unlimited point of view is best if you wish to give a more panoramic or historical account of the setting than any of your characters could possibly give.

First-Person Point of View and Setting

When describing setting or people in first-person point of view,
you must limit yourself to the information that the narrator himself
would notice. If your narrator has seen his surroundings daily for
a long period of time, for example, he may not notice the setting
unless something has recently or drastically changed. In chapter 1
of Charles Dickens's *Great Expectations*, the young narrator Pip
describes his surroundings as he saw them when he was a child.

> At such a time I found out for certain that this bleak
> place overgrown with nettles was the churchyard . . . ; and
> that the dark flat wilderness beyond the churchyard, inter-
> sected with dikes and mounds and gates, with scattered
> cattle feeding on it, was the marshes; and that the low
> leaden line beyond was the river; and that the distant savage
> lair from which the wind was rushing was the sea; and that
> the small bundle of shivers growing afraid of it all and begin-
> ning to cry was [the narrator himself] Pip.

Because Dickens is only presenting the items in the setting that
young Pip noticed, including the gravestones of his similarly
named ancestor and his infant children, we, too, feel the dread and
dismal atmosphere of the setting.

If the character would not pay particular attention to the setting and you are using first-person point of view, then you must present it as the narrator would see it himself. You have to think about your characters and their lives carefully when describing setting and using first-person point of view. Because it is always a limited point of view, you can only present setting and character description as the narrator would honestly see it.

Inner Limited Point of View and Setting

Inner limited point of view, since it is exactly like first person but uses grammatical third person, is limited in the same ways as first person. If you find either of these points of view too limiting, then you should write in unlimited.

Outer Limited Point of View and Setting

The most demanding point of view is outer limited because you must be an objective, nonjudgmental camera eye. The limitations of this point of view extend, of course, to the presentation of setting. That means if you choose this point of view, your setting must be presented as if you were merely an objective observer recording the scene.

Ernest Hemingway is a master at this point of view. Take a look at some setting description from his story "A Clean, Well-Lighted Place," written in outer limited point of view.

> They sat together at a table that was close against the wall near the door of the café and looked at the terrace where the tables were all empty except where the old man sat in the shadow of the leaves of the tree that moved slightly in the wind. A girl and a soldier went by in the street. The street light shone on the brass number on his collar. The girl wore no head covering and hurried beside him.

Notice the virtual absence of adjectives and adverbs in this setting description. That is commonplace in outer limited (see more on this point of view in chapter 6). Also, read works by Alain Robbe-Grillet to see excellent setting descriptions in outer limited point of view.

FINAL WORDS ON SETTING

Don't think of setting as something to be gotten out of the way as soon as possible. When you're using first-person or inner limited points of view, setting can lend valuable insight into your protagonist's inner life. In outer limited point of view, you can use setting to develop your characters because you cannot present their inner emotional lives. In all the points of view, setting can become almost a character in its own right and can also help you develop the human characters, themes and symbolism of your novel.

TIP Use unlimited point of view if you want to present a panoramic or historical view of the setting. When using one of the limited points of view, you must present the setting as the characters would see it (first person and inner limited) or as a camera would record it (outer limited).

DIALOGUE AND POINT OF VIEW

Once writers have mastered urgency and character development, the next major stumbling block is dialogue. The biggest mistakes that inexperienced writers make are including absolutely everything someone might say in real life (things like uh, duh, hmmm, etc.) and writing dialogue so wooden and lifeless that no human on earth would ever talk that way.

Guidelines for Writing Dialogue

Here are some general rules and suggestions for dialogue that apply no matter what point of view you're writing in.

- Aim for natural-sounding dialogue.
- Characters should talk only to each other (not to readers).
- Remember silence and actions can be as effective as words (if not more effective).
- Show characters' nature, history and conflict in their dialogue.

USING DIALOGUE WITH POINT OF VIEW

If you use simple dialogue tags, such as "he said," "she said," etc., then dialogue looks pretty similar no matter what point of

---

TIP Show conflict, characters' nature, history and relationship in dialogue to make it have urgency. Dialogue can also be used as a character development tool.

---

view it's written in. If you use adjectives and adverbs attached to the dialogue tags or use melodramatic dialogue tags, such as "he shouted venomously" or "she snarled," then you'll have to pay careful attention to your point of view. For example, how many people would say this about themselves, "No, I don't," I whispered in denial. After all, if someone is in denial, he doesn't realize that he's denying something. So you couldn't write something like this in first-person point of view. Dialogue adjectives such as those listed above most often appear in novels written in unlimited point of view.

If you're using outer limited point of view for your novel, then you shouldn't use adjectives, adverbs or even verbs in your dialogue tags that would give a subjective feel to your objective, non-judgmental presentation of the scene. For dialogue, then, follow the general guidelines of that particular point of view.

FINAL WORDS ON DIALOGUE

When dialogue reveals the characters' histories and their relationships, as well as any conflict they're having, then the reader is less likely to skim the dialogue. If you do not wish to write in unlimited point of view, most of the information you would include in what has traditionally been called exposition, or background, you can insert in the novel in dialogue. As long as you do it in a natural fashion, having the characters speaking only to each other and not to your readers, then you can get the benefits of the information provided by unlimited point of view in another point of view.

Dialogue is more than just having your characters talk to each other. It can, and should, reveal the complexities of the novel's characters and their relationships. If your readers can skip the dialogue in your novel, then you might as well take it out. No matter what point of view it's written in, your dialogue should add to the character development and the urgency in the novel.

EXERCISES FOR SETTING AND POINT OF VIEW

1. Describe your office (or some other room in your house) in unlimited point of view. Be sure to include the historical information about your desk, filing cabinets, etc. Be as descriptive as possible. Would someone seeing your office for the first time recognize it from what you have written?

2. Describe some room in your house in first-person point of view from the perspective of a pet. What would the pet notice about the room? What are the good sleeping places? Are there any toys or other interesting items that he could get into? Include only those items and spots that would interest the pet.

3. Describe some room in your house in outer limited point of view, that is, as if you were a fly on the wall or a camera, nonhuman and completely objective. Do not use any adjectives or adverbs in this exercise. Do not judge. Simply observe.

4. Describe your hand (or some other body part) in first-person point of view from the perspective of your other hand (or from the perspective of some other part of your body). How does your left hand regard the right? What does it notice about the right? How does it feel about the right hand? How does the rest of your body feel about your right hand? How would your left hand describe your right hand?

5. Do exercise 4 again, this time in unlimited point of view. If you wish, include medical terminology or other information about your hand (or body part) so that you are providing all the information possible on the hand.

6. Do exercise 4 again, only this time in outer limited point of view. Remember that in this point of view, you must not judge what you see; you must be objective.

7. Get a roll of pennies from the bank. Pick out one penny. Write a paragraph describing it in great detail using unlimited point of view. Do not cheat and write anything on the penny. Now give the paragraph to a friend. Mix the penny back with the other ninety-nine pennies from the roll. Have your friend read the description of the penny that you've written and then find the penny. If your friend finds the penny, you've written a good paragraph.

8. Do the exercise in number 7, with a different penny, in first-person point of view. Narrate the description from the perspective

of the penny. In other words, you are the penny: Be the penny. What does it feel like to be a penny? Are you happy with your life? How do you feel about dimes, nickels, quarters? What happens to you? Do not cheat and write anything on the penny. Now give the paragraph to a friend, mix the penny with the others from the roll, have your friend read the description of the penny that you've written and then find the penny. If your friend finds the penny, you're a very talented penny and have written a good paragraph.

EXERCISES FOR DIALOGUE AND POINT OF VIEW

1. Write a scene in outer limited point of view in which all the action, setting and descriptions are revealed through dialogue. Use only "he said" or "she said" for dialogue tags. That means, for example, instead of saying, "she screamed," you would use "she said" and have another character say, "My God, stop screaming, will you?" to show what tone of voice or volume level. Make sure the scene has urgency. Show the history of the characters as well as their natures and their relationship to each other—all through the dialogue itself. Show it to your readers to get their reactions and suggestions for improvement.

2. Write a scene of dialogue that takes place on the telephone, but reveal *only one side of the conversation*. That means you will have to reveal the unheard side of the conversation through the heard character's reactions and dialogue. Show it to your readers, and ask them to fill in the unheard parts of the conversation. If they are absolutely correct, then you've done a good job.

3. Write a scene with dialogue in any point of view where one character does not respond verbally to the other. This one is much like the telephone conversation exercise, only this time you can show the actions and behavior of the character who is not speaking. This is not technically a dialogue, since only one person is speaking, but it is metaphorically a dialogue since the behavior of the second character is in response to the spoken words of the first character. Show it to your readers to get their reactions and suggestions for improvement.

4. Write an entire story in any point of view in which absolutely everything takes place in dialogue: setting, conflict, urgency, character development, etc. Everything. Use only "he said," "she said"

as dialogue tags. Show it to your readers for their feedback and suggestions for improvement.

5. Watch a film you have never seen with the sound off. When the movie gets to a scene with more than one character interacting, watch it several times. Pay special attention to the body language, facial expressions and gestures of the characters. Now write the dialogue that you imagine is taking place, using outer limited point of view. Try to make your dialogue reflect the actions and emotions you see in the film.

6. Rent or watch a film you have never seen. This time, listen to the movie without watching it. When you get to a scene with dialogue, that's the scene you want. Listen to the dialogue several times—without watching the film. Now write the actions that go along with that dialogue, in any point of view. Be specific about body language, facial expressions and gestures. Include details about setting if it seems natural. Make the behavior in your scene correspond with the dialogue you heard.

7. Go to a public place and sit near a couple, a family or a group of people. Listen to what they're saying without being observed yourself (people tend to get upset if they think you're eavesdropping). Record as much of the dialogue as you can, as faithfully as you can. Now make up the characters who are speaking this dialogue and invent their lives, their histories together and the conflict (if there is no conflict already present in the dialogue). Change the dialogue if you need to make it more interesting and exciting. Write it as if it were a scene for your novel, in any point of view. Show it to your readers for their feedback and suggestions for improvement.

FOURTEEN

EROTIC SCENES, VIOLENT SCENES AND POINT OF VIEW

Each time you struggle until you master the higher level of skills you need to meet the growing demands of your book, you become more proficient and stronger as a writer.

DONNA LEVIN

Get That Novel Started!

Erotic or violent scenes are some of the most challenging scenes to write, and point of view, perspective and focus are vitally important if these scenes are to work successfully in the novel. Before you attempt to write these types of scenes, you should familiarize yourself with the principles presented in the previous chapters.

EROTIC SCENES AND POINT OF VIEW

Although many major literary works (including Boccaccio's *The Decameron*, Chaucer's *The Canterbury Tales* and Joyce's *Ulysses*) have, at times, been considered pornographic, erotic scenes and pornography are not the same thing. Pornography usually has no purpose but the sexual arousal of the reader. Erotic scenes may include sex but are about larger issues present in the work. Many beginning writers think that the fastest way to break into the best-seller market is to include gratuitous and graphic sex scenes, many of which qualify more as pornography than erotica since the scenes have absolutely no purpose other than sexual titillation. If you wish to include erotic scenes in your novel, they should be integral to the work no matter which point of view you choose.

You should, however, take genre expectations into consideration. Even within genres there is variation about presenting erotic scenes, even if all the authors are writing in unlimited point of view. In romances, for example, Amanda Quick (aka Jayne Anne Krentz) tends to use more poetic descriptions for the sexual act, as this excerpt from chapter 15 of her novel *Mistress* indicates:

> "Very well," [said the heroine]. "But I warn you, all I know of this sort of thing is what I have learned from our last experience together and what I observed during my tour of Lartmore's [pornographic] statuary hall."
>
> "It will be enough, I promise you." He cupped her with his palm and felt the moist heat that awaited him. "More than enough."
>
> "You're certain?" She ran her thumb across the end of his shaft.
>
> Marcus steeled himself. "Quite certain." He moved his fingers through the soft nest of hair between her thighs until he uncovered the swollen bud. He stroked gently.

Other romance writers, though still using unlimited point of view, are more explicit in their erotic scenes, as this excerpt from chapter 9 of Linda Howard's suspense-romance *Kill and Tell* illustrates:

> She could barely speak. His fingers reached deep inside her, pressing upward. His thumb rasped over her clitoris, circled it enticingly.

And later in that same scene:

> She kissed her way down his body. By the time she reached his groin, he was awake, erect, groaning. She kissed his shaft, licked the length of it, and felt it grow even more, then she took him fully in her mouth.

Erotic scenes can be found in any point of view, but there will be some general genre expectations and variations on the acceptable level of explicit description. Here are some basic guidelines, however, to help you when writing your erotic scenes.

Guidelines for Erotic Scenes
- Remember an erotic scene is not necessarily about sex.
- *Always* make the scene about something other than sex.

- Show the characters' history, natures and conflict through the scene, just as you would for dialogue.
- Avoid clinical description.
- Use the language your characters would use.

TIP Let your characters guide you in your choice of diction in any scene, but especially in erotic scenes, even if you're writing in unlimited point of view. What language do your characters use when thinking about the act? That's the language and diction you should use when writing about it, even if you choose to write in unlimited point of view.

FINAL WORDS ABOUT EROTIC SCENES AND POINT OF VIEW

There is a wide range of acceptable diction and details in erotic scenes, as well as variations on the types of erotic scenes that are acceptable in each genre. There are also erotic scenes depicting homosexual encounters, masturbation, voyeurism, etc. If you're writing erotic scenes in first person or inner limited, you need to maintain the character's perspective about the erotic scene, including the type of language the protagonist would use. If you're writing in outer limited, you need to remain objective, impersonal and nonjudgmental, staying out of all characters' heads. In unlimited, of course, there are no restrictions to the type of information you can present or to the vocabulary you can use in erotic scenes.

In any point of view, you should remember that "erotic" is in the eye of the beholder, so you won't be able to write an erotic scene that every reader will find erotic. The goal, therefore, should be to make it erotic for the characters who are participating in the erotic scene.

VIOLENT SCENES AND POINT OF VIEW

It's difficult to tell writers how to put violence into their novels without worrying about the moral and ethical implications of that issue. There are many who would argue that violence in art causes violence in society. Violence in art does change how we perceive violence in real life, so artists must behave responsibly when putting violence into their novels.

Sometimes, violence is absolutely essential to a novel, but violent scenes should not be gratuitous. Also, there are many types of violence besides physical violence. Just as with erotic scenes and dialogue, violent scenes must be absolutely integral to the novel's themes, character development, urgency, etc. Don't fill your novel with violence in the hopes of making the best-seller's list. Use violent scenes sparingly to make them most effective, and make sure they are inseparable from the other major elements of the novel. Otherwise, well-written violent scenes, no matter which point of view they're written in, follow many of the same guidelines that erotic scenes do.

Guidelines for Violent Scenes
- *Always* make the scene about something other than violence.
- Show the characters' history, natures and conflict.
- Remember other forms of violence, including emotional, verbal and psychological, as well as physical.
- Avoid physically graphic description.
- *Hints* of violence can be more effective than graphic depictions.

VIOLENCE AND SETTING
Another thing to take into consideration when you're doing setting is that you can use it to show violence. Setting can do more than just create atmosphere. Violent settings can be found across the genres, in both literary and commercial fiction, and in many different points of view.

Some novels that effectively use violent settings include Emily Brontë's *Wuthering Heights*, Herman Melville's *Moby Dick*, Jules Verne's *A Journey to the Center of the Earth*, Joseph Conrad's *Heart of Darkness* and *Lord Jim*, and Barry B. Longyear's *Infinity Hold*—all of which are written in first-person point of view.

Other novels with violent settings include Larry McMurtry's *Lonesome Dove*, Edgar Rice Burroughs's *Tarzan* series, William Golding's *Lord of the Flies* and Ernest Hemingway's *The Old Man and the Sea*—all written in unlimited point of view. One of the best novels on setting and violence written in outer limited point of view is Alain Robbe-Grillet's masterpiece *Jealousy*.

COMBINING EROTIC AND VIOLENT SCENES

It is possible to combine erotic and violent scenes, but there should be a specific purpose for doing so, a purpose beyond reader titillation and best-seller expectations. Many of the classics have done exactly that. The opening of Philip José Farmer's science fiction classic *Image of the Beast* is quite graphic in its depiction of the alien emasculating the human male in the act of sexual intercourse. Its graphic nature, in fact, has been labeled "pornographic" by the *Science Fiction Encyclopedia*. Since the detective viewing the "home movie" of the act was the partner of the dead man, however, he becomes more motivated to pursue the killer because of the violence of the sexual act.

In part 2, chapter 11 of Tolstoy's *Anna Karenina*, just after Vronsky and Anna have made love for the first time, the erotic scene is mingled with violent metaphors to demonstrate the guilt, pain and societal repercussions that will come from this adulterous sexual union. Tolstoy writes in unlimited point of view, making the readers aware of his own moral judgment about Anna's adulterous affair through word choices and his use of the violent metaphor for their sexual act.

There are quite a few examples of erotic and violent scenes combined, but remember that whatever guidelines are true for erotic or violent scenes separately are especially true when you combine the two. The most important one, however, would be to make the scene about something other than the sex and the violence. For further examples, see Dorothy Allison's *Bastard Out of Carolina*, Rosellen Brown's *Before and After* and Philip José Farmer's *Image of the Beast*, among others.

FINAL WORDS ON VIOLENT SCENES AND POINT OF VIEW

If you're writing violent scenes in first person or inner limited, you need to maintain the character's perspective about the violence. If you're writing in outer limited, you need to remain objective, impersonal and nonjudgmental. In unlimited, of course, there are no restrictions.

In any point of view, you should remember that "violent" is a relative term, so different readers will find different things violent. The goal should be to make the violent scenes integral to the novel so that they reveal insights about the characters who are participating in the scene.

EXERCISES FOR EROTIC SCENES

1. Write an erotic scene, in unlimited point of view, involving a piece of food, but no sex. In other words, describe the food so erotically that the reader is aroused though the character(s) with the food are not using it for sexual purposes. In fact, there may be no characters present at all. The food may be the only object in the scene. Show it to your readers. Their reactions will tell you how successful you've been. Ask them for feedback to improve the scene's erotic nature.

2. Write an erotic scene, as above, but using the food in a sexual way. (For a real challenge, do not use bananas; many authors have already done this.) Use unlimited point of view. Ask your readers for feedback to improve the scene's erotic nature.

3. Rewrite the scene in exercise 2, this time in first-person point of view, being careful to use only words and diction your narrator would use. Is it more difficult or easier in this point of view? Why? Get your readers' feedback to improve the scene's erotic nature.

4. Write an erotic scene with at least two people in which one person is unaware of the eroticism of the situation. (Think of Vladimir Nabokov's *Lolita* before Lolita realizes that Humbert is interested in her.) Use unlimited point of view. Ask your readers for feedback to improve the scene's erotic nature.

5. Rewrite the scene from exercise 4, this time in outer limited point of view. Be sure to present only the external behavior and dialogue of the characters. Show it to your readers, and ask them for feedback to improve the scene's erotic nature.

EXERCISES FOR VIOLENT SCENES

1. Write a scene in unlimited point of view in which the violence has already taken place, but write it as if you were observing a

black-and-white photograph. In other words, if there's blood in the scene, you would write about the dark stain on the kitchen linoleum or spattered on the light wall. Show it to your readers and get their reaction. Ask them for feedback to improve the scene.

2. Write a violent scene in unlimited point of view as if it were a black-and-white movie instead of a still photograph. Show it to your readers for feedback to improve the scene.

3. Write a violent scene in unlimited point of view using verbal violence/abuse instead of physical abuse. Show it to your readers for their feedback.

4. Write a violent scene in unlimited point of view using psychological or emotional violence instead of physical violence. Show it to your readers and get their feedback.

5. Write a violent scene in any point of view in which the setting itself is violent. For examples, see Aleksandr Solzhenitsyn's *One Day in the Life of Ivan Denisovich*, Willa Cather's *My Ántonia*, Meg Files's postapocalyptic *Meridian 144* and Barry B. Longyear's *Infinity Hold*. Try it with and without human characters. Show it to your readers, and ask for their feedback to improve the scene.

6. Write any of the previous violent scenes in outer limited point of view. Ask your readers for feedback.

FIFTEEN

REVISION, WRITER'S BLOCK AND POINT OF VIEW

Every story has an author and a reader, and how the story gets from one to another is at the heart of [point of view].

RUST HILLS

Writing in General and the Short Story in Particular

If you've made it to this chapter, then no doubt you have a significant portion of your own novel done. Congratulations. Now you can use point of view to revise and improve your novel, as well as to eliminate those occasional instances of writer's block.

REVISION AND POINT OF VIEW

Revision means a "new vision," and revising the novel does not mean merely editing it for grammatical mistakes or running a spell-checker. Revising a novel means having an entirely new vision for it, one that dramatically alters the novel as you now have it. That means you might eliminate characters, add characters, write a section of the novel in first-person point of view rather than in unlimited point of view, divide the novel into two first-person narratives rather than one so that another character gets to tell her perspective of the action, start the action where the novel ends by throwing away any exposition and seeing where the characters take you, etc.

The most important thing to remember when you're revising a novel is that you need to see the novel in a completely different way in order to successfully revise it. Then revision becomes an exciting part of the creative process rather than drudgery. The revision exercises included in this chapter use point of view to help you see your novel in an entirely new way.

USING POINT OF VIEW TO ELIMINATE WRITER'S BLOCK

Even the most prolific writers sometimes experience writer's block. Every writer dreads it. When you have writer's block, every word you write on the page is the wrong word, or no matter how long you sit at your desk, you can't get a single word onto the page at all. There are many outside influences that can cause writer's block: not enough sleep, overwork, not eating properly, stress, arguments with your spouse or your children, etc. There are also elements in the novel itself that can create writer's block: following a predetermined outline too rigidly, trying to force characters to do something they don't want to do, using the wrong point of view, exhausting your creative/artistic well by never taking any writing vacations, working too long on the same piece of writing, etc.

Much of writer's block is caused by not taking care of yourself: physically, emotionally or spiritually. So if you persistently experience writer's block, you might look at other aspects of your life to determine the causes. In addition to the exercises presented in chapter 10 on learning to listen to your characters and tuning into your intuition, both of which can help eliminate writer's block, you can use the exercises in this chapter to help stimulate your writing so that you eliminate writer's block.

EXERCISES FOR REVISION AND POINT OF VIEW

1. Take any scene from your novel that is giving you difficulties or that your readers say is not working for them, and rewrite it in a completely different point of view. If you have written it in first-person point of view, you might rewrite it in unlimited point of view; if you've written it in unlimited point of view, you might rewrite it in outer limited point of view. Don't just change the pronouns in this revision. Change the way you see this scene. If that revision doesn't make the scene come more alive for you and your readers, pick another point of view and redo the scene again. The goal is to find a point of view that makes the scene come alive so that it feels like it's writing itself.

2. Pick any scene of your novel written in first-person point of view, and rewrite it again in first-person point of view but from another character's perspective. Instead of looking at the scene

from Debbie's perspective, for example, look at it from Timothy's perspective. Make sure you do some of the intuition exercises for listening to your characters before you try to rewrite it from the other character's perspective. You want to explore in depth how the other character feels about the scene when you rewrite it. You can then use this information—if not the entire scene—by adding pertinent details revealed in this exercise to the novel's final draft.

3. If you're having difficulties making your characters realistic or distinguishable from one another, you might try some journal exercises written in first-person point of view from the other characters' perspectives. For example, if Richard and Susan and Kelly are having an argument, but Susan isn't a very well-developed character, you might write a first-person narrative from Kelly's perspective exploring how Kelly views Susan. What does Kelly like about Susan? What does she dislike? What does she find attractive? Unattractive? How did they first meet each other? What kind of relationship do they have? After you've learned everything you can about Susan from Kelly's perspective, do the same thing from Richard's perspective, exploring how Richard feels about Susan, asking the same questions of Richard that you asked of Kelly. These first-person narratives, because they're only journal exercises, will not be likely to end up in the final draft of the novel. However, they will give you insight into Susan's character that you may not have accessed in any other way, and you can put these insights into the novel to further develop her character.

4. Take any scene that is causing you difficulty, and eliminate all the adjectives and adverbs so that you're left only with the nouns and verbs. Reprint this scene as edited and then do not look at it for at least twenty-four hours. When you come back to the scene, now comprised of only nouns and verbs, examine whether or not this scene has the action or the effect you intended. If it does not, redo the scene's nouns or verbs to make it more powerful. Do not add adjectives or adverbs until the scene is satisfactory without them. Then if you choose to add adverbs or adjectives, do so sparingly.

EXERCISES TO ELIMINATE WRITER'S BLOCK

1. Write a letter of complaint, in first-person point of view, to your novel, telling your novel exactly how you feel about it. Are

you frustrated? If so, what is it that's frustrating you? Are you angry? Are you having difficulty finding time to work on the novel? Are your characters resisting you? Are your characters refusing to do what you want them to do? Do you feel the novel will never get revised or published? Are your family members resenting the time you spend with the novel? Do people make fun of you when you tell them you're a writer? Do you blame your novel for this? Have your readers deserted you? Put all of your negative feelings toward the novel and toward the novel-writing experience into this letter.

2. Now write your novel's response to your letter of complaint, in the form of a letter, in first-person point of view. Be sure to address all the issues you raised in your letter of complaint from exercise 1. Put the completed letter in an envelope and address it to yourself. Put a stamp on it. One day when you are experiencing writer's block, mail the letter to yourself.

3. Now write a love letter to your novel, in first-person point of view, telling your novel and its characters everything you adore about it. Is the plot simply stunning? Is the language and style sensuous and exciting? Are you absolutely in love with your characters? If so, what made you fall in love with them? Do you look forward to working on your novel every day? Do you rush home from work or get up early in the morning just so you can work on your novel? Are you proud of the novel and of how it's turning out? Do you feel more alive than you ever have because of the novel? Do you thank God every day that the novel is in your life? Put all of your positive feelings toward the novel and toward the novel-writing experience into this letter. Put the letter in an envelope, addressed to you, and mail it to yourself one day in the future when the writing is going poorly.

4. Now write your novel's love letter back to you in second-person point of view, with the novel addressing you yourself in second person. What does your novel admire about you? Your dedication? Your commitment? Your hard work? Your research skills? Your attitude? The fact that you get up an hour earlier in the morning so you can write before you go to work? Be sure to have your novel explain in great detail everything it admires and loves about you. Mail that letter to yourself (or have someone else mail it to you when you don't expect it so it'll be a wonderful, loving sur-

prise). Read the letter whenever you're feeling discouraged about the writing.

5. Keep a diary or journal recording the times you experienced writer's block. What life events or personal issues were occurring when you experienced writer's block? Is your writer's block cyclical? Hormonal? Is it influenced or caused more by external life events, or is it caused by the actual writing? If it's caused by the writing, are you trying to force your characters to do something they don't want to do? Do you need to change the point of view? Has it been too long since you've taken a vacation from the novel? Keeping the journal will, at the very least, give you a safe place to vent your frustrations about writer's block. In all likelihood, however, it will help you discover the patterns that cause writer's block; once you eliminate the patterns causing it, you can get on with your writing.

6. Take a planned vacation from your writing. If you need to write a note to your novel telling it you're going on vacation, then do so. When you're on vacation, do not think about the novel. Concentrate instead on taking care of yourself: physically, emotionally and spiritually. The vacation could be one day long, one week, one month. When you come back to the novel, you'll see it with new eyes. This will usually eliminate any writer's block you might have been experiencing.

7. Pretend you are a critic: Write a review for your novel in unlimited point of view. What are the novel's strengths? Its weaknesses? What are your suggestions for improvement?

HISTORICAL OVERVIEW AND DEVELOPMENT OF POINT OF VIEW IN LITERARY FICTION

Point of view is one of the most challenging elements of writing fiction that any author has to master, and it is impossible to become proficient at point of view without reading books written in a variety of points of view. By reading widely, you can expand your conscious as well as your intuitive appreciation for the technical aspects of point of view. Rather than simply provide a list of titles and authors, I have explained some of the important books in the following three appendices, to guide you in your choice of reading material. Appendix A covers literary works written before the modern period.

Even though you're writing contemporary fiction, it is essential that you read older fiction, drama and poetry. Some of the finest character development available can be found in older, classic works of literature. In addition, some of the innovations in point of view have appeared in earlier centuries, though these books and authors may not have received the widespread recognition of later authors. By reading some of the earlier works, you can more quickly hone your own point of view skills. Then you can acquaint yourself with the modern and contemporary literary works (appendix B) and with commerical fiction (appendix C).

Literary fiction, sometimes called literature, includes novels in which the writing style or techniques and character development are of more importance than market considerations. Unlike genre or commercial fiction, which usually follows a predictable plot pattern or formula, literary fiction has no defined rules. In fact, one of the hallmarks of literary fiction is its continual overthrowing of writing rules, traditions or conventions. Most ground-breaking techniques in point of view occur first in literary fiction since the writing style is of greater importance than sales figures; therefore, literary works more frequently contain bold innovations in point of view. In recent years, much genre fiction has imitated literary fiction in terms of point of view, changing the genres and their formulas considerably as genre authors include some of the literary point of view innovations.

ROMANCE VS. NOVEL

In European countries the term *roman* is used for the novel, linking it to the older *romance*. Traditionally, the romance is fiction, written in the vernacular rather than in Latin, with an emphasis on plot; it contains extravagant characters, remote and exotic places, heroic events, passionate love or mysterious and supernatural occurrences. The romance, with its antecedents in classical Greek literature, fully developed in France in the twelfth century and most often employed unlimited point of view. In the eighteenth and nineteenth centuries, a clearer distinction was made between novels and romances: Romances dealt with imaginatively improbable events, while novels most commonly dealt with realistic events.

THE NOVEL'S ORIGINS

The term *novel* comes from the Italian word *novella* (meaning "new little thing") after the short, broadly realistic tales popular during the medieval period and best represented by Boccaccio's *The Decameron* (1348–1353), a group of one hundred stories united by a frame story. In the outer frame story, ten people fleeing from the plague in Florence gather at a villa in the countryside. They agree that each of them will tell a story for each of the ten days of their stay. Considered a masterpiece of classical Italian prose, *The Decameron*'s sophisticated structure and writing influenced Chaucer and many Renaissance writers. *The Decameron* uses first-person point of view in the frame story and usually starts each tale with a first-person section as each character prefaces his or her tale. The tales themselves are most often in unlimited point of view, with occasional introductions of second person as the characters address their listeners.

Geoffrey Chaucer's work was influenced by Boccaccio's.

Chaucer's *The Canterbury Tales* (1387–1400) are also framed: In the outer story, pilgrims from all social classes and professions embark on a pilgrimage to the shrine of St. Thomas à Becket in Canterbury. To entertain themselves on the journey, they decide to have a storytelling contest. The plan is for each pilgrim to tell a story on the way to the shrine and on the way back. Chaucer died before completing the tales, but those we have are renowned. The twenty-four individual tales are linked by dramatic scenes involving the pilgrims, and the character development is superb.

In *The Decameron*, the ten storytellers, all of noble birth, are indistinguishable from each other. Except for one character who is slightly humorous, the narrators' voices prefacing the tales are virtually identical. Not so in *The Canterbury Tales*. Chaucer's pilgrims reveal their vivid personalities through the first-person prologues that preface their tales, as well as through their remarks and behavior as they react to the tales of the other pilgrims. The Wife of Bath, for example, whose prologue is longer than her tale, is an especially vivid example of the stunning character development Chaucer manages to include in his first-person prologues. *The Canterbury Tales* themselves—a collection of medieval types of literature, including romances, fabliau, classical legends, saints' lives, tragedies, *exemplum* (stories useful to preachers) and beast epics—are often written in unlimited point of view, with occasional inclusions of first or second person as the pilgrims comment on their own tales or as other pilgrims interrupt the teller. Also, the General Prologue to the tales, in which all of the pilgrims are described, is told to us by a naïve pilgrim, coincidentally named Chaucer, whose innocent admiration of pilgrims in the religious orders or in a higher social class reveal him to be an unreliable narrator, one not fully aware of the implications of the details or events he relates (see chapter 3 for an excerpt and additional analysis).

PICARESQUE NOVELS

One of the major influences on the development of the novel in the English language was Miguel de Cervantes's masterpiece *Don Quixote* (1605, 1615), which satirized romances and fused them with the picaresque—a chronicle presenting the life story of a rascal or rogue as he engages in the seamier underside of life. The picaresque novel is episodic in plot and appears structureless. It's romantic in the sense that it contains great adventures, but it is strongly marked by its realism. Although it is likely to be written in first-person point of view, there is virtually no character development in the picaresque novel. Even if the external circumstances of the life of the protagonist—the *picaro*—changes, such as in his inheriting a fortune or marrying extremely well, the nature of his character does not change. He remains a rogue throughout, and though he is never actually a criminal, he comes quite close to being one.

Cervantes's *Don Quixote* opens with the famous line, "At a village of La Mancha, whose name I do not wish to remember, there lived a little while ago one of those gentlemen who are wont to keep a lance in the rack, an old buckler, a lean horse and a swift greyhound." Cervantes occasionally uses first person, calling Quixote "our gentleman," but basically the novel is in unlimited point of view. Henry Fielding's *Joseph Andrews* (1742), England's first comic novel, and his masterpiece *Tom Jones* (1749) were both written in imitation of Cervantes's *Don Quixote*. Mark Twain's *The Adventures of Huckleberry Finn* (1884) is similar to picaresque novels in that its plot is episodic and the adventures are linked only by the fact that the protagonist takes part in all of them. Some readers include Huck in the *picaro* category, feeling that his essential character does not change throughout the novel. Most readers believe, however, that unlike other picaros, Huck does develop morally, especially in respect to his attitudes toward slavery and toward the escaped slave, Jim.

Some critics claim Daniel Defoe's *Robinson Crusoe* (1719) as the first fully fledged modern novel. The full title is this:

> The Life and Strange Surprizing Adventures of Robinson Crusoe, of York, Mariner: Who Lived Eight and Twenty Years, All Alone in an Un-inhabited Island on the Coast of America, Near the Mouth of the Great River Oroonoque; Having Been Cast on Shore by Shipwreck, Wherein All the Men Perished but Himself. With an Account how he was at last as Strangely Deliver'd by Pyrates. Written by Himself.

It is these last words that have the greatest significance for the development of point of view in the English novel. The earliest novels were written in the form of diaries, journals, and letters, perhaps because this was the form of writing most familiar to the authors' readers. There was also a great deal of direct address, using second-person point of view, so the audience felt intimately acquainted with the first-person narrator who was relaying the tale. Even Jonathan Swift's *Gulliver's Travels* (1726), with its bizarre and patently unrealistic adventures, purports to be an actual diary of Lemuel Gulliver, a surgeon and sea captain who visits remote regions of the world, and is written in first person.

EPISTOLARY NOVELS

While some critics tout *Robinson Crusoe* as the first English novel, others cite Samuel Richardson's *Pamela: Or Virtue Rewarded* (1740) as the first major work to combine the three elements considered characteristic of the novel genre: contemporaneity, verisimilitude and philosophical significance. (The definition of the modern novel and its characteristics determines which book is considered the first English novel.) *Pamela*, the story of a servant who avoids seduction and is rewarded in marriage, is an epistolary novel: Most of it is told through letters, so it is in first-person point of view with second person interspersed; the latter part of *Pamela*, though written as if it were a journal or diary, still addresses her parents directly, thus maintaining the pattern of first-person point of view in conjunction with second person. Epistolary novels enjoyed their greatest popularity in the eighteenth century. Perhaps the audience was more willing to accept the new novel genre because it was presented as a familiar, domestic type of writing. Along with Richardson's *Pamela* and his masterpiece *Clarissa* (1747–1748), epistolary novels include Fanny Burney's *Evelina* (1778), Madame de Staël's *Corinne, or Italy* (1807), Jean-Jacques Rousseau's *Julie, ou la Nouvelle Héloïse* (*Julie, or the New Eloise*, 1761) and Choderlos de Laclos's *Les Liaisons Dangereuses* (1782, made, in recent years, into the critically acclaimed film *Dangerous Liaisons*).

Although epistolary novels have never died out completely, there were fewer of them in the nineteenth and twentieth centuries. Some modern novelists have returned to this first-person format, most notably Bel Kaufman in *Up the Down Staircase* (1965) and Alice Walker in *The Color Purple* (1982). E. Annie Proulx altered the epistolary format into picture postcards in her novel *Postcards* (1992), while Nick Bantock and his publisher provided the actual correspondence, envelopes and postcards in his hand-lettered and drawn Griffin and Sabine series (*Griffin & Sabine* 1991, *Sabine's Notebook* 1992, *The Golden Mean* 1993). E-mail novels are probably not far behind. And telephone novels, such as Nicolas Baker's *Vox* (1992), take first person (and second person) to the phone.

DIARY AND JOURNAL NOVELS

"Diary" novels, such as Defoe's *Robinson Crusoe* and his *A Journal of the Plague Year* (1722), Swift's *Gulliver's Travels* and Edgar Rice Burroughs's *The Land That Time Forgot* (1918), all written in first-person point of view, have long been popular. Actual diaries, journals and letters, though not extended narratives, were similar to autobiographies and memoirs, which have always fascinated audiences. Many writers have taken advantage of the popularity of this intimate form of first person by writing novels that are supposedly diaries or personal journals.

AUTOBIOGRAPHIES AND MEMOIRS

Autobiographies are life stories written by the person who lived it, usually stressing the inner and private life of the author. Memoirs are a form of autobiography that usually includes personalities and actions of people other than the writer. Often the authors of memoirs have witnessed or participated in significant historical events.

The first autobiography is considered to be St. Augustine's *Confessions* (c. 400), the groundbreaking exploration of the author's philosophical and emotional development during his restless youth and his conversion to Christianity. Other famous autobiographies and memoirs include Jean-Jacques Rousseau's *The Confessions* (1782–1789), Thomas de Quincey's *Confessions of an English Opium Eater* (1821–1822), Stendahl's *Memoirs of an Egotist* (1892), James Weldon Johnson's *The Autobiography of an Ex-*

Colored Man (1912), Maxim Gorky's *My Childhood* (1913), Henry Adams's *The Education of Henry Adams* (1918), Mary McCarthy's *Memories of a Catholic Girlhood* (1957), Simone de Beauvoir's *Memoirs of a Dutiful Daughter* (1958), *The Autobiography of Malcolm X* (1965), Vladimir Nabokov's *Speak, Memory* (1966) and Frank McCourt's *Angela's Ashes* (1996).

FICTIONAL AUTOBIOGRAPHY

Some authors present their own life stories in the guise of fiction, as did Thomas Wolfe in *Look Homeward, Angel* (1929) and James Joyce in *A Portrait of the Artist as a Young Man* (1916), although Joyce's novel is written in inner limited point of view rather than in first person. Simulated autobiography is often used in fiction. Defoe used the technique in *Moll Flanders* (1722), as did Nikolai Gogol in *The Diary of a Madman* (1834), Charles Dickens in *Great Expectations* (1860–1861) and *David Copperfield* (1869), J.D. Salinger in *The Catcher in the Rye* (1951), William Styron in *The Confessions of Nat Turner* (1967) and Marguerite Duras in *The Lover* (1984).

Instead of using the autobiography format, some authors imitate biography in their novels. Gabriel García Márquez related a fictitious biography by a first-person narrator who takes on the role of a reporter in his novel *Chronicle of a Death Foretold* (1981). Jack London took simulated biographies to new levels in his novel *The Call of the Wild* (1903) and *White Fang* (1906), both of which are written in unlimited point of view. Because the protagonists of London's novels are dogs, they are sometimes erroneously categorized as children's novels.

In the Victorian period, the novel replaced poetry and drama as the most popular literary form, perhaps because the novel's social scope included characters and stories about the middle and working classes when the reading audience was comprised largely of women and servants.

GOTHIC NOVELS

Gothic novels, originated by Horace Walpole in his wonderfully quirky *The Castle of Otranto* (1764), introduced supernatural terror as well as the mysterious, awesome and sublime. Ann Radcliffe's novels, especially *The Mysteries of Udolpho* (1794), added to the popularity of the form, while her emphasis on setting and story rather than on character became the convention for this form of the novel. Mary Wollstonecraft Shelley's *Frankenstein* (1816) and Bram Stoker's *Dracula* (1897) are classic gothic novels. Both are told in first-person point of view; Shelley's is layered first-person narratives while Stoker's is a combination of diary entries and letters.

Twentieth-century novelists such as Daphne du Maurier carried on the same atmosphere of brooding and unknown terror as the gothic novels in her work *Rebecca* (1938) and *My Cousin Rachel* (1950). Patrick McGrath's works are considered masterpieces of gothic literary fiction: *The Grotesque* (1989), *Spider* (1990), *Dr. Haggard's Disease* (1993) and *Asylum* (1997). Du Maurier's and McGrath's novels are often told from first-person point of view. Mystery stories and those that invoke terror, like Edgar Allen Poe's, no matter what their point of view, are often considered derivations of the gothic novel.

Southern Gothic

The term *Southern gothic* is often used to describe a style of writing practiced by many writers of the American South whose tales are characterized by grotesque, macabre or fantastic incidents. William Faulkner (especially in stories like "A Rose for Emily"), Flannery O'Connor (*Wise Blood* 1952, *The Violent Bear It Away* 1960), Carson McCullers (*The Heart Is a Lonely Hunter* 1940, *The Member of the Wedding* 1946, *The Ballad of the Sad Café* 1951) and Truman Capote (in his early work) are the best known of the so-called Southern gothic writers.

HISTORICAL NOVELS

Historical novels, which attempt to reconstruct a past age, are most often written in unlimited point of view and were considered to be established by Sir Walter Scott in *Waverley* (1814) and *Ivanhoe* (1819). Actual figures from history often appear in such novels, sometimes interacting with the fictional characters, and major historical events form an important part of the background. The characters and plot are usually subordinated to the commentary on larger social issues, though not always, and the novel is usually written in unlimited point of view. Noted successors of Scott in the historical novel are William Makepeace Thackeray (*Vanity Fair* 1847–1848), Alexandre Dumas (*The Three Musketeers* 1844, *The Count of Monte Cristo* 1844–1845), Victor Hugo (*The Hunchback of Notre Dame* 1831, *Les Misérables* 1862), Leo Tolstoy (*War and Peace* 1865–1869, regarded by many as one of the great technical achievements in the history of the Western novel, *Anna Karenina* 1875–1877) and James Fenimore Cooper in his novels of American frontier adventure known as the Leather-stocking Tales (including *The Last of the Mohicans* 1826 and *The Deerslayer* 1841). The historical novel has also been parodied, such as in John Fowles's *The French Lieutenant's Woman* (1969); and Mark Twain, at least, felt that Cooper's Leather-Stocking novels were so historically inaccurate that they must also be parodies.

NOVELS OF MANNERS

Novels of manners emphasize social customs, manners, conventions and mores of a definite social class. Such novels are always realistic, and sometimes they are satiric and comic, as in Henry Fielding's or Jane Austen's work. Austen's work, written in unlimited point of view, concentrated on character and personality, with an emphasis on the tensions between her heroines and their society (*Sense and Sensibility* 1811, *Pride and Prejudice* 1813, *Emma* 1815). American author Edith Wharton is best known for her novels about the upper-class society into which she was born. Her classic *Ethan Frome* (1911) is written in first person, while her Pulitzer Prize-winning *The Age of Innocence* (1920) is written in unlimited point of view. John Cheever (*The Wapshot Chronicle* 1957, *The Wapshot Scandal* 1964) is sometimes considered to write novels of manners, since his work deals with the life, manners and morals of middle-class, suburban America.

POINT OF VIEW IN LITERARY FICTION

A survey of the most famous books from all categories of literary fiction reveals that all points of view appear: first, first with second, unlimited, inner limited, outer limited and many other combinations of point of view.

HISTORICAL OVERVIEW AND DEVELOPMENT OF POINT OF VIEW IN MODERN AND CONTEMPORARY NOVELS

In the modern period, literary authors have done many dramatic and experimental things with point of view, as well as with other elements of fiction, such as character development and plot. By familiarizing yourself with the more *avant garde* or dramatic innovations in point of view, you can learn which points of view you are most comfortable reading and writing, and, therefore, expand your own point of view repertoire.

You should read literary fiction even if you are writing commercial fiction. Reading good literature, no matter what the genre or the time period, will help you develop point of view, which, in turn, will help make your novel more readable and publishable. Although some earlier works (which are explained in appendix A) contained experiments with point of view, the most profilic experimentation in this area appears in modern and postmodern literary novels. Many of these works, along with analyses of the major philosophical movements which influenced or inspired their point of view experimentation, are discussed in appendix B. Much of the point of view innovations have worked themselves into commercial fiction, which is analyzed in appendix C.

Although the terms applied to literature are merely convention among critics and others who discuss literature, modern novels are usually distinguished from previous novels by their closer attention to the psychological realism of their characters, who are often much more fully developed than their earlier counterparts no matter what point of view they're written in. Contemporary novels are sometimes called postmodern; but in the late twentieth century, critics began paying more attention to literature that had previously been neglected, so there are many more categories than earlier.

PSYCHOLOGICAL NOVELS

Psychological novels concentrate more on characters and their inner lives than on plot or historical events, and literature has always been concerned with man's inner life. Geoffrey Chaucer's poem *Troilus and Criseyde* (c. 1380) has been called a psychological novel in verse, while Shakespeare's *Hamlet* (c. 1601), along with many of his other plays, has been called psychological drama. The first novel to explore the inner self was Laurence Sterne's *Tristram Shandy* (1760–1767). An experimental work in first person, with second person throughout, this novel broke all the rules and conventions developed to that point. Events do not occur in chronological order, anecdotes are often left unfinished and entire pages are filled with asterisks, dashes, line drawings, Latin text or left completely blank.

Because of his exploration of inner life, experimental though it may be, Sterne is considered one of the forerunners of psychological fiction. The term was first applied, however, to a group of novelists in the middle of the nineteenth century: George Eliot (*Adam Bede* 1859, *The Mill on the Floss* 1860, *Silas Marner* 1861, *Middlemarch* 1871–1872, considered her masterpiece), Elizabeth Gaskell (*Sylvia's Lovers* 1863, *Wives and Daughters* 1864–1866, unfinished at her death but considered her finest work) and George Meredith (*The Ordeal of Richard Feverel* 1859, *The Egoist* 1879).

American author Henry James was considered a master of the psychological novel, and his fiction (*The Portrait of a Lady* 1881, *The Wings of the Dove* 1902) and literary criticism developed many twentieth-century novel techniques. Thomas Hardy (*Far From the Madding Crowd* 1874, *Tess of the D'Urbervilles* 1891, *Jude the Obscure* 1895) and Joseph Conrad (*Lord Jim* 1900, *Heart of Darkness* 1902) were also greatly interested in psychology and influential on future writers. James's, Hardy's and Eliot's works were all written in unlimited point of view; Conrad often used first person, layering stories and employing unreliable narrators.

Émile Zola, Fyodor Dostoevsky, Herman Melville and others were also considered forerunners of the psychological novel, exploring as they did the complex inner workings of the human mind and heart. Zola's *La Bête Humaine* (*The Human Beast* 1890), written in unlimited point of view, details the emotions, thoughts and behavior of a man who could be viewed as a serial killer.

Dostoevsky is famous for his psychological penetration into the darkest regions of the human heart and has had a profound influence on the twentieth-century novel. *The Double* (1846) introduced the idea of a split personality or the divided self, a theme revisited in his *Notes from the Underground* (1864), *Crime and Punishment* (1866) and *The Brothers Karamazov* (1879–1880). Dostoevsky writes in both first-person and unlimited point of view.

Herman Melville in his masterpiece *Moby Dick* (1851) varies the point of view constantly, sometimes using first person from Ishamel's perspective, sometimes using unlimited point of view as in the whaling treatises, and sometimes using first person but switching narrators in each paragraph, as he does in chapter 99, "The Doubloon," when a multitude of characters view the gold doubloon nailed to the mast, each giving his own thoughts on the coin's significance.

Interior Monologue

In the twentieth century, with the advance of psychology and psychiatry, the psychological novel has blossomed. Many novels feature interior monologues and stream-of-consciousness passages. Interior monologues are the fictional presentation of unspoken thoughts and have their antecedents in dramatic soliloquies. Édouard Dujardin's *Les lauriers sont coupés* (literally, *The Laurels Are Cut Down*, but translated as *We'll to the Woods No More* 1887) is often cited as the first example of the use of interior monologue in a novel, though there are some passages similar to an interior monologue in Sterne's *Tristram Shandy*. The first-person narrative of letters and journals in novels could also be considered as variations of the interior monologue.

Stream of Consciousness

Stream of consciousness as a term was first applied to the mind by William James (brother of the novelist Henry) in his *Principles of Psychology* (1890), and since then it has been used to describe an author's technique of rendering the mental processes of his characters. In stream-of-consciousness passages, the author attempts a "streamlike" representation of the character's consciousness, including sensory perceptions, memories and unconscious associations as well as conscious thought. Some of the most famous stream-of-consciousness passages can be found in James Joyce's *Ulysses* (1922), Virginia Woolf's *Mrs. Dalloway* (1925) and *To the Lighthouse* (1927), and William Faulkner's *The Sound and the Fury* (1929) and *As I Lay Dying* (1930).

TIP As a narrative method, stream of consciousness allows an author to explore and exhibit to her audience even the unconscious associations and private symbols that lie beyond a character's conscious understanding. Read famous stream-of-consciousness passages, and then use stream of consciousness as a way to learn about your characters' hidden thoughts, desires and lives.

MODERN NOVELS

The modern period in fiction is considered to have started along with World War I, since that war radically and fundamentally changed the way humans in the western hemisphere viewed life. Cynicism, a profound sense of alienation and ironic detachment characterized the response to the human predicament in the Western world. Artists consciously broke with tradition—in subject matter, technique, themes and narrative form. Many writers experimented with language itself, and radical treatment of point of view altered the Western novel.

In many respects, modern literature was a reaction to the Realism and Naturalism that preceded it. Realism, with its sometimes petty attention to trivial details, and Naturalism, with its emphasis on determinism and scientific knowledge of human behavior and the laws of the universe, were themselves a reaction to the Romantic period that had preceded them. All three periods contributed to the Modern period, however.

Romanticism

Romanticism was itself a reaction to the perceived rigidity and formal orthodoxy of the NeoClassical (also called the Restoration) period, during which artistic ideals of order, symmetry, logic, restrained emotion, correctness and decorum were considered essential. Romanticism encouraged the idea of individuality and freed the writer from the restraints and rules that had marked the previous period in art. Although the Romantic period occurred at different times in Europe and the United States, there are several tendencies common to all literature classified as Romantic.

Tenets of Romanticism

- celebrates the individual
- displays strong faith in mankind's fundamental goodness and eventual perfection
- embraces nature as a model for harmony in society and in art
- is egalitarian
- stresses the value of inborn expressive abilities common to all, not needing to be developed through training

The British Romantic poets like Keats, Shelley and Wordsworth are perhaps better known than the novelists. Because Emily Brontë (*Wuthering Heights* 1847) and her sister Charlotte (*Jane Eyre* 1847) wrote at the end of the British Romantic period, they are often classified as belonging to the Victorian Age, although their works demonstrate strong Romantic tendencies. The American Romantic period occurred approximately one hundred years after the British and European phase and was much darker in tone and mood. Although English Romantic authors certainly dealt with the themes of death, loss of innocence and sadness, American Romantics seemed more obsessed with death and tended to portray nature in a more violent and negative way than did their British counterparts. American Romantic fiction writers include Herman Melville (*Moby Dick* 1851), Nathaniel Hawthorne (*The Scarlet Letter* 1850, *House of the Seven Gables* 1851) and Edgar Allan Poe.

Realism

Realism in fiction is an attempt to truthfully represent life, without embellishment or exaggeration, in a way that is observable by others. Realists often thought of their art as a mirror, objectively reporting life, and of themselves as reporters. Realism was a reaction to what were considered the excesses and self-indulgences of the Romantic period.

Realistic writers include Honoré de Balzac (*La Comédie humaine* [*The Human Comedy*] 1830, *La Cousine Bette* [*Cousin Bette*] 1946), Ivan Turgenev (*Fathers and Sons* 1862), Gustave Flaubert (*Madame Bovary* 1865), Leo Tolstoy (*War and Peace* 1865–1869, *Anna Karenina* 1875–1877), Marcel Proust (*A la recherche du temps perdu* [*Remembrance of Things Past*] 1912), George Eliot (*Adam Bede* 1859, *Middlemarch* 1872), Fyodor Dostoevsky (*Crime and Punishment* 1866, *The Brothers Karamazov* 1879–1880), Mark Twain (*The Adventures of Huckleberry Finn* 1884) and William Dean Howells (*The Rise of Silas Lapham* 1885). All these writers used various points of view, from first to unlimited, and showed the importance of realistic representation of everyday life in order to advance artistic themes.

Naturalism

Basically, Naturalism added the theories of scientific determinism to realism in art. The work and beliefs of Darwin, Freud, Marx and Calvin all contributed to the naturalist movement in fiction. Briefly, the types of determinism their theories seem to imply are as follows:

- **Darwin** emphasized the importance of biological or genetic heritage and "survival of the fittest" in determining human fate.
- **Freud** stressed the importance of the unconscious, of childhood experiences and of the sex drive in guiding human behavior.
- **Marx** emphasized the importance of socioeconomic situation and class structure in shaping human life and decisions.
- **Calvin** stressed the importance of Christianity and God's predetermination control of human life.
- **Newton** emphasized the invariability of the laws of the physical universe and their effect on human behavior.

Naturalists strive to be as objective as Realists, but they tend to be more pessimistic about human fate and behavior than do Realists. In Naturalist novels, humans are often seen as victims of fate or of forces that they cannot control (if, indeed, they are even aware of these forces). Naturalism strives to be objective and non-judgmental in its presentation of human life and frank in its portrayal of humans as creatures driven by the fundamental drives of survival, fear, hunger and sex.

French writer Émile Zola (*Thérèse Raquin* 1867, *Nana* 1880, *Germinal* 1885, *La Bête Humaine* 1890) is considered the father of Naturalism. His influential essay "Le Roman expérimental" ("The Experimental/Empirical Novel" 1880) paints the novelist as a scientist in a laboratory, testing various hypotheses with his characters and settings. English writer Thomas Hardy (*Far From the Madding Crowd* 1874, *Tess of the D'Urbervilles* 1891, *Jude the Obscure* 1895) is often considered a Naturalist, but American authors embraced the tenets of Naturalism more readily. Some of the classic American writers who are considered Naturalists are Theodore Dreiser (*Sister Carrie* 1900, *An American Tragedy* 1925), Jack London (*The Call of the Wild* 1903, *White Fang* 1906), Frank Norris (*McTeague* 1899, *The Octopus* 1901), Stephen Crane (*Maggie: A Girl of the Streets* 1893), John Steinbeck (*Of Mice and Men* 1937, *The Grapes of Wrath* 1939, *East of Eden* 1952) and, in drama, Eugene O'Neill (*Desire Under the Elms* 1925, *Mourning Becomes Electra* 1931, *The Iceman Cometh* 1946, *Long Day's Journey Into Night* 1956).

Many late nineteenth-century writers, like Flaubert, Zola, Dostoevsky and Tolstoy, whether categorized as Realists or Naturalists, are considered modern writers because of their themes, stylistic innovations or psychological insight into the human condition.

Modernism

Modern literature took many of the components of Naturalism and Realism and used them to examine the inner self. Modern writers include Joseph Conrad (*Lord Jim* 1900, *Heart of Darkness* 1902), Virginia Woolf (*Mrs. Dalloway* 1925, *To the Lighthouse* 1927), D.H. Lawrence (*Sons and Lovers* 1913, *Women in Love* 1921, *Lady Chatterley's Lover* 1928), Aldous Huxley (*Crome Yellow* 1921, *Antic Hay* 1923, *Brave New World* 1932), James Joyce (*A Portrait of the Artist as a Young Man* 1916, *Ulysses* 1922), William Faulkner (*The Sound and the Fury* 1929, *As I Lay Dying* 1930, *Absalom, Absalom!* 1936), Gertrude Stein (*Three Lives* 1909, *Tender Buttons*

1914, *The Autobiography of Alice B. Toklas* 1933), F. Scott Fitzgerald (*The Great Gatsby* 1925, *Tender Is the Night* 1934) and Ernest Hemingway (*The Sun Also Rises* 1926, *Farewell to Arms* 1929, *For Whom the Bell Tolls* 1940, *The Old Man and the Sea* 1952).

POSTMODERN NOVELS

In the postmodernist period, innovation remained an important element of fiction, but there was an emphasis on reflexivity—so that the fiction is in some way *about* fiction. Postmodern authors were probably influenced by Alain Robbe-Grillet's *For a New Novel* (1963), which meant to defend and explain the French "noveau roman" (new novel), sometimes called antinovels (see below). One of the major themes of postmodernist work is disillusionment and life's lack of meaning (or humans' inability to discover life's meaning). The alienation, historical discontinuity and absurdity of modern fiction continues in postmodern novels, with existentialism still present even in contemporary work; but postmodern fiction questions realism's assumptions that fiction can ever accurately portray real life.

Existentialism

The various philosophies (dating from about 1930) that have been referred to by the term *existentialism* have in common an interpretation of human existence in the world that stresses its problematic character. Though the ideas essential to existentialism were shared by many people before World War II, the most important existentialist philosophers only achieved worldwide recognition after the war.

Threatened by material and spiritual destruction during the war, Europe found existentialism a particularly relevant philosophy. In existentialism, the negative aspects of existence, such as pain, frustration, sickness and death, become the essential features of human reality. As a philosophical movement, it was something of a direct reaction to perceived social ills and was embraced by artists and writers as much as by philosophers. Existentialism and Absurdism are both reflected in postmodern novels.

Major Tenets of Existentialism

- The world is irrational (or, at any rate, beyond man's total comprehension).
- The world is absurd in the sense that no ultimate explanation can be given for it.
- Senselessness, emptiness, triviality, separation and inability to communicate pervade human existence, giving birth to anxiety, dread, self-doubt and despair.
- The individual confronts the necessity to choose how he is to live within this absurd and irrational world.
- Life has no meaning except what each individual gives it.

Absurdism

The philosophical and theological roots of the term *absurd* can be traced to Tertullian, an early father of the Catholic Church who argued that the surest sign of the truth of Christianity is its absurdity. He posited that the idea of an infinite deity incarnating himself and undergoing suffering for human beings is so irrational that no one would invent such a story; therefore, it must be true.

Centuries later, Søren Kierkegaard reemphasized the absurdity of Christianity; but with Martin Heidegger and Jean-Paul Sartre, absurdism became almost completely secularized. According to Heidegger and Sartre, man is thrown into an alien, irrational world in which he must create his own identity through a series of choices for which there are no guidelines or other criteria. Because man cannot avoid making choices (for to refrain from choosing is, in itself, a choice), man is condemned to be free. This absurdity is an inescapable part of the human situation. Furthermore, man's search for order and meaning in this irrational and meaningless universe brings him into conflict with that universe.

Theatre of the Absurd

One of the most significant contributions to comic drama in the twentieth century was the Theatre of the Absurd, a form of drama that emphasizes the illogical and purposeless nature of existence. The main concern of the major dramatists of the absurd is to examine a situation that epitomizes man's fundamental helplessness in a contradictory and alienating universe. Sometimes social criticism is embedded in these works, but this is less important than their portrayal of the human reaction to the essential realities of existence: death, self, time, loneliness, communication and the difficulty thereof, and individual freedom. These ancient themes are presented in ways that are intended to shock the audience. These dramas are often characterized by dark humor along with unconventional forms and subject matter. The philosophical movements of Absurdism and Existentialism, as well as the Theatre of the Absurd, had a great impact on postmodern novelists.

Absurdism, Existentialism and Postmodern Novelists

Though mostly known as a playwright, Samuel Beckett (*Waiting for Godot* 1952, *Happy Days* 1961) was tremendously influential on postmodern novelists. His characters, sometimes described as tragic clowns, seem incapable of understanding even the basic elements of life, yet symbolize all alienated and abandoned (by God) human beings. His novels (see the next page under "Antirealistic Novels") are an important part of postmodernism.

Russian-born Vladimir Nabokov (*Lolita* 1955, *Pale Fire* 1962, *Ada, or Ardor: A Family Chronicle* 1969) plays sophisticated, stylistic literary games in his novels, maintaining serious subject matter and themes but always reminding the reader that he is an author writing a book and that writing is largely self-reflexive. Beckett's and Nabokov's novels are often written in first person with insertions of second-person or unlimited points of view.

Postmodernists toy with the novel's conventions and often play complex linguistic games in their books, no matter what point of view they write in. Kurt Vonnegut (*Slaughterhouse-Five* 1969, *Breakfast of Champions* 1973, *Deadeye Dick* 1983), Thomas Pynchon (*V* 1963, *The Crying of Lot 49* 1966, *Gravity's Rainbow* 1973), Doris Lessing (*The Golden Notebook* 1962) and John Barth (*The Sot-Weed Factor* 1960, *Giles Goat-Boy* 1966, *Lost in the Funhouse* 1968) are representative of the postmodernists.

Writers like Walter Abish (*Alphabetical Africa* 1974) and Donald Barthelme (*Snow White* 1967) attack the conventions of narrative in their fiction, while authors like John Fowles (*The French Lieutenant's Woman* 1969), Margaret Drabble (*The Waterfall*

1969) and Iris Murdoch (*The Black Prince* 1973) frequently intrude into their own work to comment on it.

Authors like Günter Grass (*The Tin Drum* 1959, *Cat and Mouse* 1961, *Dog Years* 1965, *The Flounder* 1978), who includes political commentary in his self-reflexive novels, and Anthony Burgess, who invented a new language for his classic *A Clockwork Orange* (1962), continue some of the stylistic innovations begun by the postmodernists.

Metafiction

When authors write fiction that plays with the nature and process of fiction itself, it is sometimes called *metafiction*, indicating that it is above the story itself. Works included in this category include Fowles's *The French Lieutenant's Woman* (1969), Lessing's *The Golden Notebook* (1962), Barth's *Lost in the Funhouse* (1968) and most of Vonnegut's novels.

Antirealistic Novels

Antirealistic novels are the fictional counterpart to the Theatre of the Absurd, the latter of which is represented by Samuel Beckett's *Waiting for Godot*. Beckett's fiction (*Molloy* 1951, *Malone Dies* 1956, *The Unnamable* 1958) is considered the epitome of antirealistic novels. Other authors who are considered innovators in antirealism include Franz Kafka (*The Trial* 1925, *The Castle* 1926), Henry Miller (*Tropic of Cancer* 1934, *Tropic of Capricorn* 1936), Malcolm Lowry (*Under the Volcano* 1947), Thomas Pynchon, Donald Barthelme and John Hawkes (*The Cannibal* 1949). Short story writer Jorge Luis Borges, one of the more affirmative antirealists, summed up the basic philosophy of the fiction of antirealism during one of his visits to the United States: "All life is a parable, though we do not know what it means."

Antinovels

Antinovels, called "nouveau roman" or "new novels" in French, could be considered to have started in the eighteenth century with Laurence Sterne's *Tristram Shandy*, but the form has been most popular in the twentieth century. Authors of antinovels attempt to "free" fiction from the restraints, constraints and expectations concerning technique and subject matter. As a result, the novels in this category are sometimes fragmented and disordered (since the authors expect that the reader will be able to reconstruct the intended meaning). Alain Robbe-Grillet (*Les Gommes* [*The Erasers*] 1953; *Le Voyeur* 1955, *La Jalousie* [*Jealousy*] 1957) is the most well known of the antinovelists. Another famous antinovelist is Nathalie Sarraute (*Portrait d'un inconnu* [*Portrait of a Man Unknown*] 1948, *Martereau* 1953, *Le Planétarium* 1959), who discarded conventional ideas about plot, characterization, chronology and point of view.

CONTEMPORARY POSTMODERNISM

Fiction in the last part of the twentieth century has ranged from Naturalism to Romantic fantasy, from parody to magical realism. Many writers who were traditionally ignored in the academic canon have been embraced in this category. African American, Native American, Asian American and Post-colonial writers, even when they follow traditional conventions of fiction, are often considered contemporary postmodernists.

African American Literature

Though literature written by African Americans began in the eighteenth century, the term *African American* literature, also called *black literature*, came into use after the civil rights movement. Though there were many slave narratives and autobiographies written and published by African Americans in the nineteenth century, the first full-length African American novel was William Wells Brown's *Clotel, or the President's Daughter* (1853). It wasn't until the Harlem Renaissance in the 1920s that African American writing, including fiction, began to flower. James Weldon Johnson's novel *The Autobiography of an Ex-Colored Man*, originally published in 1912, was reissued in 1927; and Claude McKay's novel about a young African American soldier's return from World War I, *Home to Harlem* (1928), became a best-seller.

Richard Wright (*Native Son* 1940) explored the alienation and violence experienced by most African Americans, and other novelists at this time included Zora Neale Hurston (*Their Eyes Were Watching God* 1937) and Chester Himes, who wrote African American mysteries. Writers like Ralph Ellison (*Invisible Man* 1952, *Juneteenth* 2000), James Baldwin (*Go Tell It on the Mountain* 1953, *Giovanni's Room* 1956, *Just Above My Head* 1979), Maya Angelou (*I Know Why the Caged Bird Sings*, an autobiography written much like fiction), Ernest Gaines (*The Autobiography of Miss Jane Pittman* 1971, *A Lesson Before Dying* 1993), Pulitzer Prize-winning Alice Walker (*The Color Purple* 1982) and Nobel Prize-winning Toni Morrison (*The Bluest Eye* 1970, *Song of Solomon* 1977, *Paradise* 1998) have continued the fine literary tradition.

Native American Literature

Native American literature, sometimes called American Indian literature, has had a relatively small circulation compared to the stereotypical literature of the American West and the Indian Wars. Although many of the earliest collections were legends and myths, many autobiographies, some of which were narrated and then transcribed or translated by whites, appeared in the late nineteenth century. Early novels by Native Americans include Sophia Alice Callahan's *Wynema: A Child of the Forest* (1891) and Mourning Dove's *Cogewea, the Half Blood* (1927). Contemporary Native American authors include Gerald Vizenor (*Bearheart* 1990), Leslie Marmon Silko (*Ceremony* 1977, *Almanac of the Dead* 1991), N. Scott Momaday (*House Made of Dawn* 1968), Louise Erdrich (*Love Medicine* 1984) and Martin Cruz Smith (*Stallion Gate* 1986).

Asian American Literature

Early Asian American writing is largely autobiographical, dealing with the immigrant experience or with the conflict between the older generation of immigrants and the younger American-born generation of their children. Some of the earliest Asian American authors to receive wide readership in the United States were C.Y. [Ching-Yang] Lee (*Flower Drum Song* 1957, *The Second Son of Heaven* 1990, *Gate of Rage* 1991), Louis Chu (*Eat a Bowl of Tea* 1961) and John Okada (*No-No Boy* 1957). Contemporary Asian American fiction writers include Amy Tan (*The Joy Luck Club* 1989, *The Kitchen God's Wife* 1991), Maxine Hong Kingston (*The Woman Warrior* 1976, *China Men* 1980), Fae Myenne Ng (*Bone* 1993) and William F. Wu, who writes science fiction and fantasy.

Post-Colonial Literature

The literature of former European colonies after they have achieved independent rule is often called post-colonial literature, and some of its major themes are imperialism, national identity and the importance of native language, culture and traditions. Authors of post-colonial literature have to deal with the difficult moral challenge involved in their choice of language for their novels. They can reach a wider audience by "betraying" their own people and writing in (or being translated into) English, or they can be loyal to their own culture and traditions by settling for a smaller audience—one that already knows the dangers and frustrations of imperialism—by choosing to write in their native language. Then there is the debate over whether descendants of the imperialist class, such as Nadine Gordimer (*July's People* 1981, *My Son's Story* 1990) and Doris Lessing, both of whom are white, can be included in this category. Though they often write of the same issues treated by other post-colonial writers, the fact that they are white of European descent causes some critics to exclude them from this category.

Some of the more well-known post-colonial writers include Michael Ondaatje (*Coming Through Slaughter* 1979, *The English Patient* 1992), Anita Desai (*Clear Light of Day* 1980, *In Custody* 1984), Oscar Hijuelos (*The Mambo Kings Play Songs of Love* 1989), Vikram Seth (*The Golden Gate* 1986, *A Suitable Boy* 1993, *An Equal Music* 1999), Chinua Achebe (*Things Fall Apart* 1958), Naguib Mahfouz (*Midaq Alley* 1947, *The Thief and the Dogs* 1961, *Miramar* 1967) and Bharati Mukherjee (*The Tiger's Daughter* 1972, *Wife* 1975, *Darkness* 1985).

Another controversial issue in post-colonial literature is whether Irish writers, who are whites that have been dominated by other whites, should be included in this category. Well-known Irish writers often included with post-colonial writers are Patrick McCabe (*The Butcher Boy* 1992, *The Dead School* 1995) and Roddy Doyle (*Paddy Clarke Ha Ha Ha* 1993, *The Woman Who Walked Into Doors* 1996).

Magical Realism

Magical realism began as a Latin American literary category characterized by the incorporation of magical, fantastic or extravagant elements into otherwise realistic fiction. Magical realists include

Gabriel García Márquez (*One Hundred Years of Solitude* 1967, *Chronicle of a Death Foretold* 1981, *Love in the Time of Cholera* 1985), Laura Esquivel (*Like Water for Chocolate* 1989), Jorge Luis Borges (sketches and stories) and Isabel Allende (*The House of the Spirits* 1982, *Eva Luna* 1987). Recently, magical realism has become an international trend, with books such as Toni Morrison's *Paradise* following the Latin American tradition.

POINT OF VIEW IN MODERN AND CONTEMPORARY LITERARY FICTION

A survey of the most famous books from all categories of literary fiction reveals that all points of view appear: first, first with second, unlimited, inner limited, outer limited and many other combinations of point of view.

HISTORICAL OVERVIEW AND DEVELOPMENT OF POINT OF VIEW IN COMMERCIAL FICTION

Many literary authors shun commercial fiction, not realizing how much exciting experimentation and point of view innovation can be found there. Much of the craft of writing can be learned by reading good books of every catagory, and many books which are considered literary are also commercial, such as George Orwell's classic *1984*. Though books classified in genres include some formulaic conventions, there is much to be learned about point of view from commercial novels. Even if you don't wish to write commercial fiction, you can learn about point of view from novels that are traditionally classified into genres for market consideration. Since the plot is of paramount importance in commercial novels, all writers can learn good plotting strategies by reading these novels. Literary authors might also benefit from studying the successful commercial novels, incorporating some of their fiction techniques into their own literary works to make them more marketable. Commercial authors will benefit from acquainting themselves with the different genres explored in appendix C as well as with the literary works discussed in appendices A and B.

Commercial fiction, also called genre fiction or popular novels, is literature with widespread appeal, identified in terms of familiar or formulaic story structures. Commercial literature is plot driven, that is, the developing plot action is the most important aspect of the novel. According to Deborah Knight in "Making Sense of Genre," characters in commercial fiction are "identified functionally, in terms of their role in a particular story structure, rather than psychologically" and such characters have "immediately identifiable moral qualities." In commercial fiction, moral judgments are often made by the author and passed on to the readers.

Rarely is there any moral ambiguity in commercial fiction, no matter what the category or genre.

In earlier societies and cultures, before the printing press, such popular literature can be identified in folktales. In more contemporary societies, popular literature is still present, and the archetypes that appeared in folktales, such as clearly identifiable "good guys" and "bad guys," now appear in genre literature. Commercial fiction appeals to large segments of society. In the nineteenth and twentieth centuries, commercial fiction has been extremely financially lucrative for its writers.

Commercial fiction is often divided into categories, or genres, such as Westerns, science fiction, romance, mystery, etc. Usually, each genre follows a specific formula, so commercial fiction is sometimes called formula fiction; but within each genre there are usually many subdivisions, each with its own formula within the larger genre formula.

SCIENCE FICTION NOVELS

Science fiction novels are based on new or futuristic scientific facts, assumptions or hypotheses. Sometimes the stories take place in the future, on other planets or in other dimensions of time and space. Though Robert Paltock's *The Life and Adventures of Peter Wilkins* (1751) conducts a war in the air with beautiful bat people, and though Mary Shelley's *Frankenstein* was predicated on scientific speculation, Jules Verne is often labeled as the true originator of modern science fiction. His groundbreaking work included *A Journey to the Center of the Earth* (1864), *20,000 Leagues Under the Sea* (1869) and *Around the World in Eighty Days* (1873). H.G. Wells's *The Time Machine* (1895), *The Invisible Man* (1897) and his famous *The War of the Worlds* (1898) further strengthened the genre.

Renowned authors Isaac Asimov (*I, Robot* 1950, the *Foundation* trilogy 1951–1953), Ray Bradbury (*The Martian Chronicles* 1950, *The Illustrated Man* 1951, *Something Wicked This Way Comes* 1962), Arthur C. Clarke (*Childhood's End* 1953), Robert Heinlein (*Methuselah's Children* 1958, *Starship Troopers* 1959, *Stranger in a Strange Land* 1961, *I Will Fear No Evil* 1970, *Time Enough for Love* 1973), Frank Herbert (the *Dune* series 1965–

1985) and Ursula K. Le Guin (*The Left Hand of Darkness* 1969, *The Dispossessed* 1974) added moral import as well as the consequences of genetic and environmental manipulations to the technical and scientific musings of science fiction.

Science fiction is broken into too many subgenres to list here, but some of the most common, with some of their authors, are listed below.

Alien Novels

Alien novels include, obviously, aliens. Sometimes they have come to earth while at other times the humans have gone to the other planets. Sometimes they are encountered in space, on the spaceship or in the space station. Kurd Lasswitz's *Two Planets* (1897) is sometimes considered the first novel describing the contact between humans and extraterrestrial beings. Other classics from this subgenre include H.G. Wells's *The War of the Worlds* (1898), Robert A. Heinlein's *The Puppet Masters* (1951), Arthur C. Clarke's *Childhood's End* (1953) and Robert Silverberg's *Nightwings* (1969).

Time Travel Novels

These novels involve travel to another time, past or future. H.G. Wells's *The Time Machine* (1895) may have been the first in this subgenre. Other authors include David Gerrold (*The Man Who Folded Himself* 1973), Isaac Asimov (*The End of Eternity* 1955), Gregory Benford (*Timescape* 1980) and Brian Aldiss (*Frankenstein Unbound* 1973, *Dracula Unbound* 1991).

This category can include the protagonists' discovering lost lands or lost races. Authors in this subgenre include H. Rider Haggard (*King Solomon's Mines* 1885, *She* 1887, *Allan Quatermain* 1887), Arthur Conan Doyle (*The Lost World* 1912), Edgar Rice Burroughs (*The Land That Time Forgot* 1918) and Henry Kuttner (*Valley of the Flame* 1964).

Alternate Worlds Novels

Alternate worlds novels are based on the premise that some moment in time or some historical event, if changed, would have a profound impact on history as we know it. Edmund Lawrence's *It May Happen Yet* (1899), in which Napoleon invades Britain, may have begun this subgenre. Many authors and historians have written nonfiction essays or books on this premise, such as G.M. Trevelyan, Alfred Toynbee and Sir Winston Churchill. The common subdivisions of this subgenre involve World War II having been won by the Axis powers or the American Civil War having been won by the South. Authors who have written this subgenre include Philip K. Dick (*The Man in the High Castle* 1962), Brad Linaweaver (*Moon of Ice* 1968), Harry Turtledove (*The Guns of the South* 1992), Robert Harris (*Fatherland* 1992) and Paul J. McAuley (*Pasquale's Angel* 1994).

Cyberpunk Novels

Coined from the title of the novel by Bruce Bethke, cyberpunk novels sometimes involve near-future worlds with the equivalent of teenaged gangs. Other times they include hackers and computer wizards/geniuses as the protagonists. Most are marked by the gritty realism and the underside of life that characterizes hardboiled detective fiction. Author Bruce Bethke is included in this category, as are William S. Burroughs (*Naked Lunch* 1959), Anthony Burgess (*A Clockwork Orange* 1962), Ben Bova (*Exiled From Earth* 1971), Philip K. Dick (*A Scanner Darkly* 1971, *Do Androids Dream of Electric Sheep?* 1968), William Gibson (*Neuromancer* 1984, *Burning Chrome* 1987, *Mona Lisa Overdrive* 1988) and Walter Jon Williams (*Hardwired* 1986, *Voice of the Whirlwind* 1987, *Angel Station* 1989).

Space Travel Novels

Space travel novels feature visits to other planets, moons, stars, comets, etc. This is a huge category, but some of the more famous authors are Robert A. Heinlein (*Universe* 1951, *Between Planets* 1951), Ben Bova (*Millennium* 1976), Greg Bear (*Moving Mars* 1993), Edgar Rice Burroughs (*A Princess of Mars* 1917, *The Gods of Mars* 1918, *Fighting Man of Mars* 1931), Kim Stanley Robinson (*Mars* trilogy 1992–1997, *Icehenge* 1984, *The Memory of Whiteness* 1985) and Jeffrey A. Carver (*Neptune Crossing* 1994).

FANTASY NOVELS

Unlike science fiction, which is predicated on scientific theory or accomplishments, fantasy literature consciously breaks free from reality. These novels depend on strangeness of setting or of characters, such as supernatural or unnatural beings, and violate natural law as we know it. Like other genre fiction, fantasy novels are often subdivided into genres, some of which are described here.

Heroic/Sword and Sorcery Novels

These types of books are based on legends or on heroes, heroines, kings and queens. Magic is present, sometimes prominently, and the hero often travels from one locale to the other. Modern sword and sorcery fiction began in the pulp magazines with Robert E. Howard's work (*Conan* stories 1932–1936). Contemporary versions of chivalric or Arthurian romances, such as the T.H. White novels (*The Sword in the Stone* 1939, *The Once and Future King* 1958, *The Book of Merlyn* 1977), are sometimes grouped into this category. Other writers in this subgenre include Marion Zimmer Bradley (*The Shattered Chain* 1975, *The Mists of Avalon* 1982), Doris Piserchia (*Star Rider* 1974, *Earthchild* 1977, *Spaceling* 1979), Joanna Russ (*Alyx* 1977, *Kittatinny: A Tale of Magic* 1978) and Thomas Burnett Swann (*The Day of the Minotaur* 1966, *How the Mighty Are Fallen* 1974, *Lady of the Bees* 1976).

Supermen novels, featuring protagonists with powers that make them superhuman, are sometimes included as a division of this subgenre. H.G. Wells's *The Food of the Gods* (1904) and Philip Wylie's *Gladiator* (1930, considered by some as the inspiration for the comic strip *Superman)* are examples of this group.

Animal Novels

Animal novels feature animals or insects with the ability to speak, sometimes with humans, sometimes only with other animals or insects. Many children's novels are included in this category. Some of the classic novels in this subgenre include Pierre Boulle's *Monkey Planet* (1964, filmed as *Planet of the Apes*), Robert Merle's *The Day of the Dolphin* (1967), Douglas Adams's *The Hitchhiker's Guide to the Galaxy* (1979), E.B. White's *Stuart Little* (1945) and *Charlotte's Web* (1952), Dick [Ronald Gordon] King-Smith's Babe books (*The Sheep-Pig* 1983, filmed as *Babe; Ace: The Very Important Pig* 1990) and Richard Adams's *Watership Down* (1974).

Magical Worlds Novels

Magical worlds novels feature magical worlds unconnected to our own. J.R.R. Tolkien's *Lord of the Rings* trilogy (1954–1956), set in the Third Age of Middle Earth, forms the sequel to his fantasy classic *The Hobbit* (1937). Other writers in this subgenre include Piers Anthony (*The Magic of Xanth* series 1977–2000), L. Frank Baum (*Oz* books 1900–1908), Ursula K. Le Guin (*The Earthsea* trilogy 1968–1973), Patricia McPhillip (*The Riddlemaster* trilogy 1976–1979) and J.K. Rowling (the *Harry Potter* series 1997–2000).

Prehistoric worlds novels, such as those featured in Jean M. Auel's *The Clan of the Cave Bear* series (1980–1990), are sometimes classified here.

Utopia/Dystopia Novels

Named after Sir Thomas More's book *Utopia* (1516), utopia/dystopia novels were actually present in a different genre as early as Plato's *Republic*. Some utopian literature attempts to describe new world orders notable for their contrast to the societal order of the time of their writing, such as More's did. Some attempt to define religiously or philosophically ideal communities, such as did Nathaniel Hawthorne's *The Blithedale Romance* (1852), while others attempt to set up utopian societies based purely on economic principles, as did Edward Bellamy's *Looking Backward* (1888). James Hilton's *Lost Horizon* (1933) and Charlotte Perkins Gilman's feminist *Herland* (1915) are examples of utopian literature. Some utopian literature ridicules current conditions but offers no solutions, such as Jonathan Swift's *Gulliver's Travels* (1726), Voltaire's *Candide* (1758) and Samuel Butler's *Erewhon* (1872).

H.G. Wells's *The Island of Dr. Moreau* (1896), Aldous Huxley's *Brave New World* (1932) and George Orwell's *1984* (1949), with their bitter depictions of antiutopian worlds, gave rise to the term *dystopia*, Greek for "bad place." Margaret Atwood's *The Handmaid's Tale* (1985) and Glenda Adams's *Games of the Strong* (1982), along with many films such as *Logan's Run* and *Gattaca*, are classic examples of dystopian stories. Sometimes utopian/dystopian literature is classified with fantasy and sometimes with science fiction, as are Robert A. Heinlein's *Have Space Suit, Will Travel* (1958) and Isaac Asimov's *I, Robot*.

WESTERN NOVELS

Stories of cowboys and gunslingers of the American frontier first arose in the dime novels and pulp fiction, then developed into Western novels. Westerns are usually written according to a simple formula, with the characters conventionalized and the actions stylized, sometimes leading to stereotypes. The lone cowboy or town marshal facing the deadly confrontation with the outlaws on behalf of innocence and justice has become an American archetype. Owen Wister's *The Virginian* (1902) and Walter Van Tilburg Clark's *The Ox-Bow Incident* (1940), however, took the Western formula but produced literature of substantial worth. Zane Grey and Louis L'Amour are prolific writers of Westerns. In the last thirty years, Larry McMurtry (*Horseman, Pass By* 1961, filmed as *Hud* 1963; *Lonesome Dove* 1985 and *Streets of Laredo* 1993) is one of the most notable contemporary writers of the Western genre.

POPULAR ROMANCE NOVELS

Romance novels, as the term is used in the twentieth century, are love stories, typically set in glamorous or exotic surroundings, with feminine chastity and virtue as a frequent theme. Most often, the young heroine falls in love with a darkly brooding, handsome, wealthy, mature man. Though troubles may follow, the romance most often ends happily in marriage. Charlotte Brontë's *Jane Eyre*, with its innocent governess falling in love with the brooding and mysterious Mr. Rochester, could be considered an archetype for this type of novel. Popular romances are subdivided into many categories, some of which, with a few of the authors, are listed below.

Contemporary/Mainstream Romances

Contemporary/mainstream romances are set in a contemporary period and locale, though the locale may be exotic. Sometimes paranormal romances are included in this category by reviewers. Writers in this category include Jude Deveraux (*The Enchanted Land* 1978), Elizabeth Lowell (*Midnight in Ruby Bayou* 2000),

Nora Roberts (*True Betrayals* 1995), Barbara Delinsky (*The Vineyard* 2000), Linda Howard (*Shades of Twilight* 1997), Joy Fielding (*The First Time* 2000), Robyn Carr (*Deep in the Valley* 2000), Dee Holmes (*The Caleb Trees* 2000), Mechelle Avey (*A Lifetime Loving You* 2000), Nell Brien (*Lioness* 2000), JoAnn Ross (*Fair Haven* 2000) and Judith McNaught (*Night Whispers* 1998).

Historical Romances

Romances of this type are set in a past age. Writers in this category include Judith McNaught (*Until You* 1995), Jude Deveraux (*Velvet Promise* 1995), Catherine Coulter (*The Heir* 1996), Julie Garwood (*For the Roses* 1996), Kathleen E. Woodiwiss (*The Flame and the Flower* 1996, *Petals on the River* 1997), Geralyn Dawson (*Sizzle All Day* 2000), Jacquie D'Alessandro (*Whirlwind Wedding* 2000), Tori Phillips (*Halloween Knight* 2000), Margo Maguire (*Dryden's Bride* 2000), Sorcha MacMurrough (*Call Home the Heart* 2000) and Madeline Hunter (*By Possession* 2000).

Regency Romances

A subgenre of the historical romance, regency romances are set during the Napoleonic Wars and Regency England. Jane Austen's work (*Sense and Sensibility* 1811, *Pride and Prejudice* 1813, *Emma* 1815) is sometimes included as the archetype of this subgenre, though she was writing contemporary romances during her lifetime. Georgette Heyer (*The Convenient Marriage* 1934, *The Spanish Bride* 1940, *The Quiet Gentleman* 1951) is credited with inventing the modern regency romance.

Contemporary regency writers include Martha Kirkland (*An Uncommon Courtship* 2000), Judith A. Lansdowne (*Lord Nightingale's Love Song* 2000), Barbara Hazard (*The Wary Widow* 2000) and Melinda McRae (*Miss Chadwick's Champion* 2000).

Americana Romances

Another subcategory of historical romances, Americana romances are set in periods and locales of America's history, including the pioneer period, the American West, the frontier era, the Civil War and the Indian territories. Writers in this category include Leslie LaFoy (*Maddie's Justice* 2000), Stephanie Mittman (*A Heart Full of Miracles* 2000), Beverly Jenkins (*Always and Forever* 2000), Kate Donovan (*Game of Hearts* 2000), Amanda Harte (*North Star* 2000), Samantha Lee (*Angel's Gold* 2000), Selina MacPherson (*A Scandalous Bride* 2000), Liz Ireland (*Trouble in Paradise* 2000), Miriam Grace Monfredo (*Sisters of Cain*, combining suspense and Americana, 2000) and Georgina Gentry (*Warrior's Honor* 2000, *Eternal Outlaw* 1999, *Apache Tears* 1999).

Science Fiction/Fantasy Romances

These novels combine romance and science fiction or fantasy elements in roughly equal quantities. Authors include Judith Tarr (*Kingdom of the Grail* 2000), Martha Wells (*Wheel of the Infinite* 2000), Janine Ellen Young (*The Bridge* 2000), Carol Berg (*Transformation* 2000), Terry Goodkind (*Faith of the Fallen* 2000), Andre Norton and Sasha Miller (*To the King a Daughter* 2000) and L.E. Modesitt (*Scion of Cyador* 2000).

Futuristic Romances

Futuristic romances feature otherworld settings and often have interstellar travel. Writers include Nora Roberts (writing as J.D. Robb, *Naked in Death* 1995, *Glory in Death* 1995, *Vengeance in Death* 1999), Jayne Castle (aka Jayne Ann Krentz, *After Dark* 2000) and Dara Joy (*Knight of a Trillion Stars* 1997).

Time Travel Romances

These novels have the modern hero or heroine somehow travelling through time to meet the dream partner. Writers include Jude Deveraux (*A Knight in Shining Armor* 1990), Diana Gabaldon (*Outlander* 1991, *Dragonfly in Amber* 1993, *Drums of Autumn* 1997), Madeline Baker (*Unforgettable* 2000), Kimberly Raye (*Midnight Fantasies* 2000), Terri Brisbin (*The Queen's Man* 2000) and Linda Howard (*Son of the Morning* 1997).

Paranormal Romances

Novels in this subcategory include elements of fantasy that can range from light (containing, for example, fantastic creatures) to dark and gothic (containing more horror elements, for example, werewolves, witches, ghosts, etc.). Authors include Susan Krinard

(*Once a Wolf* 2000), Adrienne Burns (*Three's a Charm* 2000), Lisa Cach (*Of Midnight Born* 2000), Tracy Fobes (*Daughter of Destiny* 2000), Karin Huxman (*Entangled* 2000) and Brenda Joyce (*House of Dreams* 2000).

Mystery/Espionage/Suspense/Thriller Romances

Novels in this category involve a crime, murder or mystery, and solving that crime, involve espionage and spies, or contain suspense elements as well as the traditional romance elements. This category includes writers such as Laurien Berenson (*Unleashed* 2000, *Hush Puppy* 2000), Thomas William Simpson (*The Editor* 2000), Val McDermid (*A Place of Execution* 2000), Margaret Coel (*The Spirit Woman* 2000), M.T. Jefferson (*In the Mood for Murder* 2000), Carolyn Hart (*White Elephant Dead* 2000), Sidney Sheldon (*The Sky Is Falling* 2000), Eben Paul Perison (*The Seventh Sin* 2000), Mary Freeman (*Bleeding Heart* 2000), Robert S. Levinson (*The James Dean Affair* 2000), Ellen Hart (*Slice and Dice* 2000), M.C. Beaton (*Agatha Raisin and the Witch of Wyckhadden* 2000), Carole Nelson Douglas (*Catnap* 1993, *The Cat and the Jill of Diamonds* 2000) and Mary Higgins Clark (*The Anastasia Syndrome* 1989, *A Cry in the Night* 1994, *The Cradle Will Fall* 1995, *Before I Say Good-Bye* 2000).

Inspirational Romances

Inspirational romances feature Christian or Jewish heroines or heroes who are religiously and spiritually devout. Writers in this category include Kathleen Morgan (*Woman of Grace* 2000), Rene Gutteridge (*Ghost Writer* 2000), Cindy McCormick Martinusen (*Winter Passing* 2000), Jane Orcutt (*The Living Stone* 2000), Patricia Hickman (*Katrina's Wings* 2000) and Linda Windsor (*Not Exactly Eden* 2000).

African American/Multicultural Romances

This subgenre features heroines or heroes who are African American or of another ethnic or cultural descent. Reviewers sometimes classify multicultural romances with contemporary or mainstream romances. Writers include Dorothy Elizabeth Love (*And Then Came You* 2000), Sinclair Lebeau (*So Amazing* 2000), Tamara

Sneed (*Love Undercover* 2000), Jacquelin Thomas (*Family Ties* 2000), Monica Jackson (*Heart's Desire* 1998, *The Look of Love* 1999, *Never Too Late for Love* 2000), Carmen Green (*Endless Love* 2000), Loure Bussey (*Twist of Fate* 1998, *Love So True* 1999, *Images of Ecstasy* 2000) and Sandra Kitt (*Adam and Eva* 1985, *Family Affairs* 1999, *Close Encounters* 2000).

MYSTERY NOVELS
The mystery genre encompasses crime novels, detection novels, thrillers, techno-thrillers and spy novels. Mysteries include suspense elements to keep the reader involved. Many of the books in this category involve the readers' attempt to solve the crime. Like romance and science fiction, the mystery genre is subdivided into many categories, each with its own formula and specifications for plot and character development.

Legal Thrillers
Legal thrillers feature lawyers as the protagonists and often involve trials and extensive social commentary. Harper Lee's classic *To Kill a Mockingbird* (1960) is one of the earliest archetypes of this mystery subgenre. Other writers include John Grisham (*The Firm* 1991, *The Client* 1993, *The Partner* 1997, *The Street Lawyer* 1998), Erle Stanley Gardner (*The Case of the Sulky Girl* 1933), Steve Martini (*Undue Influence* 1994) and Scott Turow (*Presumed Innocent* 1987, *The Burden of Proof* 1990, *Pleading Guilty* 1993).

Forensic Thrillers
This category features the crime-solving aspects of pathology, psychology and behavioral analysis, trace evidence processing, ballistics, etc. Sometimes these thrillers are included in the police procedural categories. Thomas Harris's *The Silence of the Lambs* (1988), P.D. James's *Death of an Expert Witness* (1977), Patricia Cornwell's *Postmortem* (1991) and Ridley Pearson's work (*Undercurrents* 1988, *Probable Cause* 1990, *No Witnesses* 1994) are often placed into this category.

Police Procedural Thrillers
These novels include realistic depictions of official investigations, emphasizing teamwork, administrative and bureaucratic difficulties

and endless paperwork. This is usually an American genre and includes the same type of gritty realism and street-life details of the hard-boiled detective fiction. Ed McBain (the *87th Precinct* series) is considered a master of police procedurals. Some of the other writers who have written this type of thriller include Eleanor Taylor Bland (*Gone Quiet* 1994), Patricia Cornwell (*Hornet's Nest* 1996), Jeffery Deaver (*The Bone Collector* 1997, *The Coffin Dancer* 1998), Tony Hillerman (*Skinwalkers* 1988, *Sacred Clowns* 1993), Elmore Leonard (*Glitz* 1985, *Freaky Deaky* 1988, *Pronto* 1993, *Out of Sight* 1996) and Lawrence Sanders (*The Second Deadly Sin* 1977).

Historical Mysteries/Thrillers

Books in this category take place in an earlier time period and include significant period details. Historical personages may also appear. Sometimes these are combined with time travel so that the detective goes backward in time to prevent an event from occurring; sometimes they are classified with alternate histories, in which the world portrayed is different from our contemporary world because some significant historical event has or has not occurred, such as the assassination of J.F. Kennedy's not taking place or Hitler's surviving World War II. Lillian de la Torre's *The Detections of Dr. Sam Johnson* (1960) and Walter Mosley's *Devil in a Blue Dress* (1990) are considered classics in this subgenre.

Military Thrillers

Military thrillers feature protagonists from the armed services, and the setting may include a war or armed military conflict. Most of these novels are also included in the espionage or police procedural categories. Techno-thrillers are often in this group since these novels contain elaborate descriptions of weaponry, the specifications of which are often relevant to the plot. Nelson DeMille's *The General's Daughter* (1992), Alistair MacLean's *Ice Station Zebra* (1963) and Tom Clancy's *The Hunt for Red October* (1984) are considered archetypes of this category.

African American Mysteries/Thrillers

These books feature African American characters as the protagonists, who range from detectives and reporters to physicians and

FBI agents. Chester Himes (*The Real Cool Killers* 1959, *The Crazy Kill* 1959, *Cotton Comes to Harlem* 1965, *Run Man Run* 1966, *The Heat's On* 1966) was one of the earliest writers in this subgenre. Contemporary authors include Tracey Tillis (*Flashpoint* 1997, *Final Act* 1998, *Final Hour* 1999), Valerie Wilson Wesley (*When Death Comes Stealing* 1994, *Where Evil Sleeps* 1996, *Easier to Kill* 1998), Gary Phillips (*Violent Spring* 1994, *Perdition, USA* 1996, *Bad Night Is Falling* 1998) and Eleanor Taylor Bland (*Dead Time* 1992, *Slow Burn* 1993, *Done Wrong* 1995, *See No Evil* 1998, *Tell No Tales* 1999).

Science Fiction Mysteries/Thrillers

This subgenre combines the elements of crime fiction and science fiction. This is a small category and includes Philip K. Dick's *Do Androids Dream of Electric Sheep?* and Isaac Asimov's *The Naked Sun* (1957).

Espionage/Spy Thrillers

Espionage/spy thrillers always include spies and spying, sometimes in the political arena and at other times in the corporate arena. Some books in this category have little sex and brief violence, but others are sex-filled and action-packed. The protagonists are not always heroes, but they usually have noble ideals. One of the earliest novels in this category was Joseph Conrad's *The Secret Agent* (1907). W. Somerset Maugham's semifictional account of his own World War II adventures in *Ashenden, or the British Agent* (1928) is sometimes considered the first realistic spy novel. John Le Carré (*The Spy Who Came in From the Cold* 1963, *Tinker, Tailor, Soldier, Spy* 1974), Ian Fleming (*Casino Royale* 1953, *Diamonds Are Forever* 1956), Helen MacInnes (*Above Suspicion* 1941), Ken Follett (*Eye of the Needle* 1978) and Graham Greene (*Our Man in Havana* 1958, *The Third Man* 1950) are considered masters in this subgenre. Michael Crichton (*Disclosure* 1994) and Tom Clancy (*Debt of Honor* 1994) have also written in this category.

Suspense Novels and Thrillers

This is a vaguer category, including novels that basically do not fit neatly into any of the other categories. Thrillers often have more action and adventure; they typically have strong male protagonists. Sometimes they have political overtones, such as Richard Condon's *The Manchurian Candidate* (1959). Suspense novels tend to be darker in tone, with a threatening atmosphere. Writers in this subgenre include Mary Higgins Clark (*Pretend You Don't See Her* 1997), Elizabeth George (*A Great Deliverance* 1988, *Well-Schooled in Murder* 1990), Frederick Forsyth (*The Day of the Jackal* 1971, *The Odessa File* 1972), Jack Higgins (*The Eagle Has Landed* 1975), Stephen Dobyns (*The Church of Dead Girls* 1997) and Joy Fielding (*The Deep End* 1993, *See Jane Run* 1996, *Missing Pieces* 1997).

DETECTIVE NOVELS

The detective genre is distinguished from the mystery genre in that the detective novel presents all the clues to the reader at the same time they are presented to the detective and that the detective logically solves the crime from a reading of these clues. The modern detective stories, with the detective solving a crime, usually a murder, by logically assembling and interpreting evidence, began with Edgar Allan Poe's tales. He introduced the first fictional detective, Auguste C. Dupin, in "The Murders in the Rue Morgue" (1841) and detailed Dupin's further exploits in "The Mystery of Marie Roget" (1842) and "The Purloined Letter" (1845). Poe was one of the first to turn the mystery story's focus from the shocking event itself to a study of the criminal mind. Earlier authors such as Charles Dickens and Wilkie Collins influenced Poe. Collins's *The Moonstone* (1868) is sometimes called the first English detective novel.

In the earlier examples of this genre, the detective was often an amateur whose mental prowess and idiosyncratic imagination allow him to solve a mystery that baffles professional policemen. Sir Arthur Conan Doyle's brilliant detective Sherlock Holmes turns crime-solving into a science with his formidable intelligence, while his down-to-earth sidekick, Dr. Watson, who narrates the stories, keeps Holmes's intelligence from intimidating readers. Agatha Christie (*Witness for the Prosecution* (drama) 1953, *Murder on the Orient Express* 1933, *Death on the Nile* 1937) is probably one of the best-known mystery writers. Dorothy L. Sayers (*The Unpleasantness at the Bellona Club*

1928, *Strong Poison* 1930) made significant contributions to the detective genre and was one of the most popular writers of her time. Other writers in this category include Nicholas Meyer (*The Seven-per-cent Solution* 1974), Rex Stout (*Too Many Cooks* 1938, *Three Witnesses* 1955) and Kate Ross (*Cut to the Quick* 1993, *Whom the Gods Love* 1995, *The Devil in Music* 1997).

Hard-Boiled Detective Fiction

Dashiell Hammett (*The Maltese Falcon* 1930, *The Thin Man* 1934) added violence, sex, tough language and gritty realism to the detective story, creating a subgenre called hard-boiled fiction. This subgenre of detective fiction is a tough, unsentimental style of American crime writing characterized by impersonal, nonjudgmental presentation of violent incidents, by an unemotional tone and by an absence of moral judgments. Hard-boiled fiction often takes place among criminals rather than among crime-fighters.

In this subgenre, the detective was sometimes changed to a private investigator, without the admirable qualities found in earlier heroes, making the protagonists more like antiheroes. Though these protagonists are usually tough, hard-edged men, they often live by strict codes of honor. Raymond Chandler (*The Big Sleep* 1939, *Farewell, My Lovely* 1940) and Ross MacDonald continued this hard-boiled tradition. Mickey Spillane's work (*I, the Jury* 1947) contained extreme sensationalism and blatant sadism, turning the genre into what *Ellery Queen's Mystery Magazine* called the "guts-gore-and-gals-school" of writing.

The cynical tone of the hard-boiled private eye's voice has also appeared in female protagonists: Sara Paretsky's private investigator V.I. Warshawski, Sue Grafton's Kinsey Millhone and Patricia Cornwell's medical examiner-turned-detective Kay Scarpetta, are all sometimes included in the hard-boiled category. Lawrence Block (*The Specialists* 1969), Elmore Leonard (*52 Pick-Up* 1974) and Derek Raymond (*How the Dead Live* 1986) are among contemporary writers in this category. Most hard-boiled detective fiction is written in first-person point of view, with the voices of the narrators making the protagonists memorable and controversial.

Noir Detective Fiction

Noir detective fiction is considered a subdivision of the hard-boiled genre. In these novels, the protagonist is usually not a detective. Sometimes he is a victim, suspect or perpetrator. Often he is tied directly to the crime, as in James M. Cain's work (*The Postman Always Rings Twice* 1934, *Double Indemnity* 1936). An emphasis on sexual relationships is another characteristic of this subgenre. The tough, gritty realism and first-person narration of hard-boiled detective fiction is often present in noir fiction. Horace McCoy's *They Shoot Horses, Don't They?* (1935) is another early noir work. Innovative noir writer Jim Thompson provided his readers with an intimate portrait of a psychotic mind (*The Killer Inside Me* 1952) and with an unusual dual ending (*A Hell of a Woman* 1954). Charles Williams's *Man on the Run* (1954) has one of the great examples of the "chase"—common in noir fiction—where the plot involves the protagonist running from the police while attempting to clear himself of a crime. Thompson's and Williams's work are written in first-person point of view. Peter Rabe (*A House in Naples* 1956, *Kill the Boss Good-By* 1956) is considered a master of unlimited point of view noir. Cornell Woolrich uses multiple points of view in his classic *I Married a Dead Man* (1948) and also leaves the identity of the murderer ambiguous.

HORROR NOVELS

Atmosphere is extremely important in horror fiction, since one of the most important components in this genre is the sensation of fright it elicits from the reader. Many books categorized in this genre also appear in other genres such as crime, gothic or supernatural fiction. The work of Andrew Vachss, for example, is often classified as modern horror and modern crime fiction since he deals with dark issues such as gay-bashing (*Choice of Evil* 1999), predatory pedophiles (*Sacrifice* 1991) and domestic stalking (*Safe House* 1998).

Although some subgenres of horror include extremely detailed depictions of physical violence, more horror authors write about the darker aspects of life without the gore, concentrating on disturbing the readers' emotions rather than their stomachs. H.P. Lovecraft, sometimes called the father of modern horror, Ambrose

Bierce, Edgar Allan Poe and Joyce Carol Oates (*Bellefleur* 1980, *Zombie* 1995) are sometimes listed as horror authors. Gothic classics such as Mary Shelley's *Frankenstein*, Bram Stoker's *Dracula*, Henry James's *The Turn of the Screw* and Daphne du Maurier's *Rebecca* are frequently classified as gothic horror.

At times, a particular work is considered a horror classic though the author himself is not counted as a horror writer. Such is the case with William Peter Blatty's *The Exorcist* (1971), Ray Bradbury's *Something Wicked This Way Comes* (1962), Ira Levin's *Rosemary's Baby* (1967) and Richard Matheson's *I Am Legend* (1954). When authors write predominantly in this genre, they are usually classified as horror writers, as is the case with Anne Rice (*Interview With a Vampire* 1976, *The Vampire Lestat* 1985, *The Queen of the Damned* 1988), Stephen King (*The Shining* 1977, *Misery* 1987, *Dolores Claiborne* 1993, *Insomnia* 1994) and Peter Straub (*Ghost Story* 1979, *Mr. X* 1999).

Intensely graphic or noir horror writers include Clive Barker (*Books of Blood* 1984–1986) and John Shirley (*Black Butterflies* 1998). New gothic, which concentrates on inner states of mind, includes literary writers such as Joyce Carol Oates, Patrick McGrath (*The Grotesque* 1989, *Spider* 1990, *Dr. Haggard's Disease* 1993, *Asylum* 1997), and Dean Koontz (*Intensity* 1996, *Sole Survivor* 1997, *Fear Nothing* 1998).

POINT OF VIEW IN COMMERCIAL FICTION

Contrary to the myth that states that all commercial fiction must be written in unlimited point of view, a survey of the most famous books from all categories of commercial fiction reveals that, as with literary fiction, all points of view appear: first, first with second, unlimited, inner limited, outer limited and many other combinations of point of view.

GLOSSARY

Allusion: A reference to something famous or well known, usually for the purposes of description and character development.

Ambiguous unlimited point of view: A variation of unlimited point of view, where multiple possibilities of interpretation for a character's behavior are presented without the author's guidance in selection, as in the work of the postmodernists.

Antagonist: The principal opponent or foil of the main character in a drama or narrative.

Antihero: A protagonist of a drama or narrative who is notably lacking in heroic qualities.

Archetype: A primordial image, character or pattern of circumstances that recurs throughout literature, myths, folklore and religious tales, and thought consistent enough to be considered universal. The term was adopted by literary critics from the writings of the psychologist Carl Jung, who formulated a theory of the collective unconscious.

Characters, evolving: Characters who change during the course of the piece of literature.

Characters, flat: Characters who are one-dimensional, i.e., like cartoon characters; a flat character cannot be evolving since his changing would indicate that he is more fully developed, like round characters.

Characters, round: Characters who are three-dimensional, i.e., like real human beings; a character who is round (fully developed) can still be static if he doesn't change throughout the course of the work.

Characters, static: Characters who do not change during the course of the piece of literature.

Combo point of view: Sometimes called limited omniscience or flexible/revolving third person, written in grammatical third person: he, she, it, they; in which the author moves back and forth among unlimited and inner limited points of view; now sometimes recognized as a distinct category by literary critics and considered conventional in some types of commercial fiction, with unlimited point of view used for the crime-fighting protagonists and inner limited for the victims or the criminals.

Comedy: A genre of literature which, though it may treat serious issues and conflicts, reaches a happy or joyful conclusion.

Conflict: The opposition of persons or forces upon which the dramatic action depends, usually categorized as man vs. man, man vs. self, man vs. nature and man vs. supernatural.

Determinism: The theory that man's destiny is shaped by some outside (or unconscious) force, whether religious, natural, economic, political or psychological. Determinism is the polar opposite of free will.

Determinism, Darwinian: The theory that natural laws of survival and biological selection shape what happens in a person's life, after the theories of naturalist Charles Darwin.

Determinism, Freudian: The theory that subconscious psychological forces and/or childhood events and/or the sex drive shape what happens in a person's life, after the theories of psychologist Sigmund Freud.

Determinism, Marxist: The theory that economic situation (or social class) shapes what happens in a person's life, after the theories of Karl Marx.

Determinism, religious: The theory that God shapes what happens in a person's life. Also called Calvinism, after the teachings of John Calvin.

Determinism, scientific: The theory that the natural laws of the universe (such as those of gravity and inertia) shape what happens in a person's life, sometimes called Newtonian determinism, after the theories of Sir Isaac Newton.

Existentialism: A movement in philosophy and literature which states that life has no meaning except what each individual gives it; some philosophers, such as Jean-Paul Sartre, believed that such freedom (to make choices) is an "awful responsibility" while others, such as Albert Camus, believed that such freedom held the potential for each man to choose to become content.

First-person point of view: A narrative method in which the story's events are related from the thoughts, feelings and observations of one character, the narrator, who tells the story using "I" or "we"; narrators may be reliable or unreliable.

Flashback: A literary technique that involves interruption of the chronological sequence of events by interjection of events or scenes of earlier occurrence, often in the form of reminiscence.

Foreshadowing: A hint of what is going to happen later in the story.

Framed story: A complete story within another story; Boccaccio's *The Decameron*, Chaucer's *The Canterbury Tales* and Fannie Flagg's *Fried Green Tomatoes at the Whistle Stop Cafe* are examples.

Free will: The theory that man has control over his own life and fate.

Inner limited point of view: A narrative method like first person in that it relates the story's events from the inner life of one character, telling the story from one person's perspective, but written in grammatical third person—he, she, it, they—used frequently by James Joyce and Henry James, among others.

Irony: Sometimes described as a secret between the author and the reader, which the character(s) in the story does not know.

Metaphor: An implied comparison, more challenging and complex than simile's stated comparisons.

Multiple points of view: Any combination of different points of view, with sections of the novel (or story) written in completely different points of view, such as a novel that combines first-person sections with unlimited sections, first and second with unlimited or unlimited with outer limited. Because the combination of unlimited point of view for the crime-fighting protagonists of a novel and inner limited for the victims or the criminals has been recognized as a separate category by critics and become conventional in some crime novels, it is listed under combo point of view.

Narrator: The "I" or the "we" telling the story, found only in first-person point of view.

Narrator, reliable: One who truthfully, correctly and reliably relates events.

Narrator, unreliable: One who does not understand the full import of a situation or one who makes incorrect conclusions and assumptions about events witnessed and related.

Naturalism: A theory in literature emphasizing the role of heredity and environment upon human life and character development (contains assumptions of scientific determinism).

Outer limited point of view: A narrative method limited to the presentation of the outer lives of all the characters in the work, presenting only that which can be seen and heard, i.e., observed from outside all the characters; no characters' thoughts or unspoken motivations are related; also called "fly-on-the-wall" or camera point of view; practiced by Ernest Hemingway and Alain Robbe-Grillet, among others.

Persona: A mask the author uses to make commentary on events both inside and outside her novel (not to be confused with the author herself or with a story's narrator).

Plot: The plan, main events of or what happens in a literary work; also known as the narrative structure.

Plot, chronological: A narrative whose events happen in a time-ordered sequence.

Plot, episodic: A narrative whose events seem disconnected to each other, such as in Cervantes's *Don Quixote* or De Foe's *Moll Flanders*, where the protagonists are the only unifying element in the novels' plots.

Plot, nonchronological: A narrative whose events do not happen in a time-ordered sequence.

Protagonist: The principal character in a novel, short story, drama or poem.

Realism: The theory or practice in art of fidelity to nature or real life without idealization (used critically to denote excessive preoccupation with trivial detail).

Romanticism: A literary, artistic and philosophical movement emphasizing the individual, the imagination and the emotions.

Second-person point of view: A narrative method that addresses a "you" (not in dialogue between characters), which may be the readers themselves; humanity in general; other actual or implied characters in the novel; or specific historical, political or otherwise famous people outside the novel who are not the readers.

Setting: The location, time, area, etc., in which a story takes place.

Simile: A stated comparison using "like" or "as."

Stream of consciousness: A narrative technique in fiction intended to render the flow of impressions, thoughts, memories and sense perceptions in the consciousness of an individual; the term was first used by the psychologist William James; this technique is sometimes called "interior monologue" and examples have been written in first-person, unlimited or inner limited points of view; used by Henry James, William Faulkner, Virginia Woolf and others.

Symbol: Something that stands for or suggests something else; it has an independent meaning from the rest of the narrative in which it appears; can have multiple meanings.

Symbol, cultural: One whose meaning is limited to an individual culture, i.e., it does not cross cultures; wearing white to a funeral to celebrate reincarnation, as they do in India, is an example.

Symbol, literary: One that frequently appears in art; some examples are snow or rain representing death, guns or cannons representing phalluses, caves representing wombs, etc.

Symbol, universal: One whose meaning crosses cultures and is understood worldwide; the swastika representing Nazis or the crucifix representing Christianity are examples.

Theme: The dominant idea(s) of a work of literature.

Tragedy: A genre of literature that deals with serious issues and themes and that reaches a sorrowful or disastrous conclusion.

Tragicomedy: A genre of literature that combines serious and lighter issues and themes, usually with the serious aspects predominating.

Unlimited point of view: Also known as the omniscient or "author as God" point of view, written in grammatical third person: he, she, it, they; where every character's thoughts, feelings, motivations, history and actions are presented; there are no limits to the information an author can reveal to his readers.

Urgency: What keeps the reader reading; could be related to plot, character development or voice.

BIBLIOGRAPHY

African American Mystery Page. 28 June 2000. www.aamystery.com.

Bate, Walter Jackson. *Criticism: The Major Texts.* San Diego, CA: Harcourt Brace Jovanovich, 1970.

Burroway, Janet. *Writing Fiction: A Guide to Narrative Craft.* New York: HarperCollins, 1996.

Cohn, Dorrit. *The Distinction of Fiction.* Baltimore, MD: Johns Hopkins University Press, 1999.

————. *Transparent Minds: Narrative Modes for Presenting Consciousness in Fiction.* Princeton, NJ: Princeton University Press, 1978.

ClueLass [Mystery fiction]. 28 June 2000. www.cluelass.com.

Defining Hardboiled Fiction. 28 June 2000. www.webfic.com/mysthome/themes.htm.

Dibell, Ansen. *Elements of Fiction Writing: Plot.* Cincinnati, OH: Writer's Digest Books, 1988.

Frey, James N. *How to Write a Damn Good Novel, II: Advanced Techniques for Dramatic Storytelling.* New York: St. Martin's, 1994.

Frye, Northrop, et al., eds. *The Harper Handbook to Literature.* 2nd ed. New York: Longman-Addison-Wesley, 1997.

Genette, Gérard. *Narrative Discourse Revisited.* Trans. Jane E. Lewin. Ithaca, NY: Cornell University Press, 1983.

Goleman, Daniel. *Vital Lies, Simple Truths: The Psychology of Self-Deception.* New York: Simon & Schuster, 1985.

The Gothic Literature Page Bibliography: The English Gothic Novel, 1764 to 1834. 30 June 2000. http://members.aol.com/ gothlit/gothicbib.html.

Guran, Paula. "A Century of Horror." *Horror Online.* 30 June 2000. www.horroronline.com/db/C/century _in_ horror/index.html.

Hall, Oakley. *The Art and Craft of Novel Writing.* Cincinnati, OH: Story Press, 1989.

Hardboiled Heaven [Detective fiction]. 28 June 2000. http://writer89.tripod.com.

Harmon, William, and C. Hugh Holman. *A Handbook to Literature.* 7th ed. Upper Saddle River, NJ: Prentice-Hall, 1996.

Hemley, Robin. *Turning Life Into Fiction: Finding Character, Plot, Setting and Other Elements of Novel and Short Story Writing in the Everyday World.* Cincinnati, OH: Story Press, 1994.

Hills, Rust. *Writing in General and the Short Story in Particular.* Rev. ed. New York: Houghton Mifflin, 2000.

Horror Writers Association. 30 June 2000. www.horror.org.

Kershner, R.B. *The Twentieth-Century Novel: An Introduction.* Boston: Bedford Books, 1997.

Knight, Deborah. *Making Sense of Genre.* 5 May 2000. www.hanover.edu/philos/film/vol_02/knight.htm.

Lamarque, Peter. *Fictional Points of View.* Ithaca, NY: Cornell University Press, 1996.

Lanser, Susan Sniader. *Fictions of Authority: Women Writers and Narrative Voice.* Ithaca, NY: Cornell University Press, 1992.

———. *The Narrative Act: Point of View in Prose Fiction.* Princeton, NJ: Princeton University Press, 1981.

Levin, Donna. *Get That Novel Started! (And Keep It Going 'Til You Finish).* Cincinnati, OH: Writer's Digest Books, 1992.

———. *Get That Novel Written! From Initial Idea to Final Edit.* Cincinnati, OH: Writer's Digest Books, 1996.

Merriam Webster's Encyclopedia of Literature. Springfield, MA: Merriam-Webster, 1995.

Moffett, James, and Kenneth R. McElheny, eds. *Points of View: An Anthology of Short Stories.* Rev. ed. New York: Mentor-Penguin, 1996.

Mystery Greats. 28 June 2000. www.mysterynet.com.

MysteryGuide.com. 28 June 2000. www.mysteryguide.com.

Nicholls, Peter, ed. *Science Fiction Encyclopedia.* Garden City, NY: Doubleday, 1979.

Novakovich, Josip. *Fiction Writer's Workshop.* Cincinnati, OH: Story Press, 1995.

The Novel. 21 June 2000. http://academic.brooklyn.cuny.edu/ english/melani/cs6/novel.html.

Olson, Barbara K. *Authorial Divinity in the Twentieth Century: Omniscient Narration in Woolf, Hemingway, and Others.* Lewisburg, PA: Bucknell University Press, 1997.

Payne, Johnny. *The Elements of Fiction Writing: Voice & Style.* Cincinnati, OH: Writer's Digest Books, 1995.

Rice, Philip, and Patricia Waugh. *Modern Literary Theory: A Reader.* London: Edward Arnold, 1989.

Riffaterre, Michael. *Fictional Truth.* Baltimore, MD: Johns Hopkins University Press, 1990.

Robbe-Grillet, Alain. *For a New Novel: Essays on Fiction*. Trans. Richard Howard. Freeport, NY: Books for Libraries Press, 1965.

Romance Novels and Women's Fiction. 26 June 2000. www.writepage.com/romance.htm.

Romantic Times Magazine. 27 June 2000. www.romantictimes.com.

Schofield, Dennis. *Second Person Fiction*. 13 March 2001. www.curtin.edu.au/curtin/dept/CCS/creative-writing/yous_lot/you.html.

Science Fiction Romance. 26 June 2000. http://members.aol.com/sfreditor.

Stewart, Garrett. *Dear Reader: The Conscripted Audience in Nineteenth-Century British Fiction*. Baltimore, MD: Johns Hopkins University Press, 1996.

Tuttle, George. *Noir Fiction [Detective fiction]*. 28 June 2000. www.geocities.com/soho/suite/3855.

———. "What is Noir?" *Noir Fiction [Detective fiction]*. 28 June 2000. www.geocities.com/soho/nook/7522.

The Ultimate Science Fiction Web Guide. 28 June 2000. www.magicdragon.com/UltimateSF/thisthat.html.

Warhol, Robyn R. *Gendered Interventions: Narrative Discourse in the Victorian Novel*. New Brunswick, NJ: Rutgers University Press, 1989.

"What's Hot in Romance: Reviews." *Romantic Times Magazine*. September 2000 (issue #199).

INDEX

Absurdism, 183
Adventures of Huckleberry Finn, The, 4, 169
Ambassadors, The, 63
Ambiguous unlimited point of view, 30-32, 207
Animal Farm, 28
Anna Karenina, 3, 22, 158
Antinovels, 185-186
"Araby," 106
Ashes to Ashes, 93-94
Audience
    discussing, in grammatical third person, 74-75
    feedback from, 17-18
    helping, with changing points of view, 118
Author
    as God, 23
    intrusive, 40-41
    vs. persona, 38-43
    voice, 124-125
Autobiographical narratives, 55, 171-172

Barthelme, Donald, 72
"Big Two-Hearted River," 83
Blue Eyes, Black Hair, 85
Boccaccio, Giovanni, 167
Body Lovers, The, 38
Booth, Wayne C., 45
Bright Lights, Big City, 68, 73-74
Brontë, Charlotte, 68
Brontë, Emily, 104-105
Brothers Karamazov, The, 4
Burgess, Anthony, 107-108

Call of the Wild, The, 28, 33
Canterbury Tales, The, 43-44, 168
Casino Royale, 26-27
Catcher in the Rye, The, 55
Cather, Willa, 45
Cause of Death, 120
Cervantes, Miguel de, 24-25, 168-169
Character(s)
    exercises, 131
    realistic, 142-143
    traditional categories, 139-141

    voice of, 124
Character development
    exercises, 143-145
    in literary vs. commercial fiction, 141-142
    and point of view, 139, 143
    and urgency, 134-135
Chaucer, Geoffrey, 43-44, 167-168
Children, as narrators, 103-104
Christie, Agatha, 47
Church of Dead Girls, The, 37
Clark, Walter Van Tilburg, 50
"Clean, Well-Lighted Place, A," 148
Clockwork Orange, A, 107-108
Combo point of view, 7, 20, 90-91, 94-95, 207
    advantages and disadvantages of, 91-92
    in commercial fiction, 93
    exercises, 95
    in literary fiction, 92-93
Commercial fiction, 14, 190-191
    character development in, 141-142
    combo point of view in, 93
    first-person point of view in, 38
    genres and subgenres, 191-206
    inner limited point of view in, 63
    moral judgment in, 22-23
    multiple points of view in, 116
    outer limited point of view in, 86
    second-person point of view in, 76-77
    unlimited point of view in, 25-27
Contemporary fiction, 175
    genres and subgenres, 176-189
    second-person point of view in, 75-76
    See also Commercial fiction
Contemporary postmodernism, 186-189
Cornwell, Patricia, 119-120
Creative writing exercises, 128-129
Crichton, Michael, 54

Death of Iván Ilých, 136
Decameron, The, 167-168
Defoe, Daniel, 169
Dialogue, 149-150
    exercises, 152-153
Diary narratives. *See* Journal and diary narratives